Hypnotic Coaching

Hypnotic Coaching

Shaun Brookhouse

and

Fiona Biddle

UK Academy of Therapeutic Arts and Sciences Ltd.

Published by

UK Academy of Therapeutic Arts and Sciences Ltd
16 St Philips Rd, Burton on the Wolds, Loughborough, LE12 5TS
Tel: 01509 881811
Email: info@ukacademy.org
Internet: www.ukacademy.org

ISBN 0-9544604-0-5

Note
Neither the publishers nor the authors will be liable for any loss or damage
of any nature occasioned to or suffered by any person acting or
refraining from acting as a result of reliance on the material contained in
this publication.

Printed in the UK by Lightning Source

Dedication

I would like to thank my parents for all their love and support throughout my life. They have been my coaches, fulfilling all the roles detailed in this book (except "formal" hypnosis", and I don't remember ever signing a contract!). Kathleen and Keith, thank you. I love you

I would like to dedicate my part of this book to two of my closest and dearest friends and colleagues. Dr Dwight Damon, President of the National Guild of Hypnotists, has been a mentor to me for a number of years. I believe that his work with the NGH will be recognised as some of the most significant in the establishment of the profession of hypnotism. Elsom Eldridge, Jr. is the convention director for the "World's largest and friendliest hypnosis conference", but he is much more than that. He is a great friend with whom I can always talk and laugh. Also, as Executive Director of the International Guild of Professional Consultants and Coaches, he is taking these burgeoning fields and making them into professions to be proud of. They have always been supportive of me both professionally and personally and I can only thank them from the bottom of my heart.

Contents

About the Authors

Shaun Brookhouse

GCGI, MA, DCH, CertEd, ACoT, DHyp, DipProfCouns, HPD, CPC, DNGH, FRSA, FNCH

Shaun has been in professional practice since 1989. He is an award winning hypnotherapist, receiving some of the most prestigious honours and Fellowships in the profession, including the Rexford L North Memorial Trophy for Life Time Achievement from the National Guild of Hypnotists.

Shaun is a Board Certified Hypnotist, a Certified Master Instructor with the National Guild of Hypnotists, a past Chairman of the National Council for Hypnotherapy (UK) and the UK Confederation of Hypnotherapy Organisations, a Certified HypnoCoach, and a NLP Master Trainer. He is the Director of Brookhouse Hypnotherapy Ltd, and Principal of the UK Academy of Therapeutic Arts and Sciences.

Fiona Biddle

BSc, DipCouns, DipCAH, HPD, CPC, FNGH, FNCH

Fiona has been in professional practice since 1993. She is a hypnotherapist, counsellor and professional coach. She also co-developed a new model of therapy: the Motivational Model of Hypnotism. Fiona is Chair of the National Council for Hypnotherapy, Vice-Principal of the UK Academy of Therapeutic Arts and Sciences, ex-Chair of the UK Confederation of Hypnotherapy Organisations and in 2002 was one of the 8 practitioners chosen to serve on the Technical Working Group to write the government approved National Occupational Standards for Hypnotherapy.

She has co-authored the books (with Shaun) "Building a Successful and Ethical Therapy Practice", and "Motivational Hypnotism".

Fiona was the 2004 recipient of the NGH President's Award

Foreword

Out of need comes innovation, brilliance, and purpose. In a changing world, the professions of coaching and consulting have re-defined themselves. Within the past decade alone, they have surged forward in growth and acceptance in ways nearly unimaginable only a few years ago.

Once the word, "consultant" was too often merely a synonym for, "recently laid off from my job; haven't yet found other work." Today the word consultant defines one who has chosen to take the reins of his or her own career; and someone who values the opportunity to grow in knowledge, professional flexibility, and income potential, free of the limitations imposed by others.

Among those careers benefiting most from these types of growth and transformational opportunities, are both hypnotism and coaching. These are two fields that stand at the forefront of consulting, yet until now, have been linked only by a fine, thin thread. Hypnotists, in their ever-expanding advancement and development, have searched for ways to bring more services and more support to their clients. At the same time, life coaches have increasingly recognized and turned to hypnotism as a powerful tool to assist clients in solving problems, reaching goals, and sticking to resolutions.

From this need, Shaun Brookhouse and Fiona Biddle have crafted an innovative blueprint, which brilliantly clarifies how the objectives of hypnosis and personal coaching can stand together. They have purposefully created new tools and new models of service. To the good fortune of the thousands of certified professionals who will use their techniques, and the perhaps millions of individuals who will benefit from them, Brookhouse and Biddle now share their blueprint within the pages of Hypnotic Coaching.

The professional reputations of Shaun Brookhouse and Fiona Biddle precede them as successful transformation facilitators—remarkably successful. As a result of their combined thirty-plus years of industry experience, they are able to draw tight cause-and-effect conclusions, leading to tight cause-and-effect solutions. I know of no other book that provides such a useful arsenal of cross-profession techniques, with the path to "stickability" so well-defined and well-designed.

Studying and implementing the working models within these covers can move the caring coach and the caring hypnotist, and his or her clients, to the "next level." Hypnotic Coaching is purely innovation, brilliance, and purpose.

Elsom Eldridge, Jr, EdM
Executive Director, International Guild of Professional Consultants and Coaches
Author: "How to Position Yourself as The Obvious Expert"

Introduction

We have been running coaching training courses since 2002, and hypnotherapy training courses since 1996. Most of our coaching students have been qualified hypnotherapists who have wanted to add coaching to their practices.

We have always encouraged them to utilise their skills in hypnotism while working with coaching clients, but have not, until now, brought the two models together explicitly. This book does just that. It is designed to equip hypnotherapists to coach their clients, and specifically to add Hypnotic Coaching to their repertoire.

Of course, we do encourage you to take our course as well! The practical value of trying out exercises in a safe environment is clear, but we will ensure that this book covers every topic to a level that is in-depth enough for you to gain confidence to use them in the real world, with real clients.

Money Magazine has referred to Coaching as the "highest paid home based business": and that's without the added tool, and credibility of hypnosis!

NB. This book is not designed to teach you to be a hypnotist or hypnotherapist. If you are not already qualified to the level laid down by the major professional bodies in your country (UK: trained on a course that is designed to meet the National Occupational Standards and/or a member of a body with standards equal to the National Council for Hypnotherapy. US: trained to the requirements of the National Guild of Hypnotists), then please see Appendix A for details of how to go about this.

What is Hypnotic Coaching?

Let's start by looking at what coaching is, and then add in the "hypnotic" bit.

What is coaching?

- An interactive relationship between two people
- A partnership where both contribute to finding the answers for the client
- A sharing of
    - resources
    - wisdom
    - insight
    - processes
    - advice
- Dependent on the needs of the client: they know what is best for them
- Challenging: always ask the client for more than they are comfortable to give
- Stretching: push your clients to learn to achieve the impossible
- Supportive
- Encouraging of self-reliance
- Holistic: the client is a whole person and no aspect should be ignored unless the client insists
- Goal orientated, but remember goals are ever changing; they will emerge and alter during the process
- Based around growth and strength, giving the client a strong base from which to take action
- Not just the session: coaching is more effective if it allows the client to act outside the session

The coaching process

- Support your clients to
  - be more
  - achieve more
  - feel better
- Encourage organisation so that they can fit in all they need
- Coach the whole client, including:
  - work
  - family
  - relationships
  - spirituality
  - finances
  - leisure
- Help them to realise that all areas are related to each other and work on one can impact on another without necessarily addressing an issue
- Be creative
- Look at causes of problems, not just symptoms
- Ask more of the client than they have been asked before, or differently, encouraging choice and expectation. If you are out of line, they will let you know if you have set up the relationship correctly
- Use your intuition, but check it out
- Discourage dependence
- Build ground in all areas of their lives
- Remember your growth and development too: this will impact on your clients
- Use reframing
- Unlock the client's potential and abilities
- Experiment
- Support the Nike ad: just do it
- Teach your clients
- Advise, but do not insist that they take your advice
- Be positive, exuberant, loving, passionate
- Be a navigator

- Offer assessment
- Be curious, always
- Let go of results
- Avoid preconceptions
- Be neutral and do not absorb their stuff
- Lead by following

Why the need for hypnotism?

Hypnotism adds a lot to the coaching process. Have a look back over the bullet points in the two sections above. Is there any element there that is not aided by the use of hypnotism? To put it simply, by incorporating hypnotism, you will be helping your client to move more quickly, think and process more clearly and from a more "real" place, to face up to blocks more readily and thus to get far more from every step of the coaching process.

Now, of course we are not saying that EVERYTHING in Hypnotic Coaching is done in trance! Some discussions as to goals, blocks, progress etc are done as normal one to one discussions, but any process that involves any depth of work is better done in trance.

Why be a Hypnotic Coach?

As you are reading this book, we can presume that you are already a qualified hypnotherapist. Are you in practice? Are you doing as well as you would like? Why did you take your hypnotherapy qualification?

The following list of reasons may well cover your reasons for becoming a hypnotherapist, and all are just "more so", with the addition of coaching to your portfolio:

- Do you want to be your own boss and work your own schedule?
- Are you a positive person? And does negativity bug you?
- Do you find it easy to connect naturally with people?
- Would you like to inspire?
- Do you like being in control? And would you like to help others to be in control?
- Are you ready for success, excellence and fulfilment?
- Are you looking for meaning, a better balance, and satisfaction in life?
- Do you want to remove barriers to your client market, and be available to the whole world, whether they need "therapy" or not?

If you answer yes to any of these, then adding Hypnotic Coaching to your practice could help you achieve your goals.

Tenets of coaching

Responsibility

Many of your coaching clients will start from a place of taking inadequate and/or inappropriate responsibility. They may take not enough responsibility, or too much. Here are examples of things they may say to indicate this issue:

- It's not my fault I eat too much, my boss insists I take clients to lunch
- I feel guilty that my husband got caught speeding
- I've tried everything to stop smoking
- I'm just disorganised; it's how I've always been
- I'm sorry you didn't like what I cooked (this sort of phrase could be ok or not depending on the tone of voice etc)
- I only hit you because you made me so angry
- I didn't mean to make you feel sad
- It's my parents fault that I haven't got a degree as they wouldn't let me go to University

The coach's task is to move the client to a place where they take responsibility for what is theirs and let go of responsibility for what is not.

This, however, is not an absolute. As a student on this course you are likely to be happy to hear the statement that your arrival at this point in your life is the result of all the choices that you have made, all the actions you have taken and all the situations you have avoided. But most clients will not initially be ready to hear this. As you know, however, it can be easier to talk to clients about tricky issues such as this while they are in hypnosis. You have an opportunity to break down these barriers much more quickly than does a coach who does not use hypnosis.

Some people have stronger beliefs about responsibility than others. Do you agree with the following? (These are given as examples and do not necessarily reflect the views of the authors)

- Each individual is responsible for all their actions, whatever the circumstances
- A person chooses their path in life before conception
- The body is completely under the control of a person's mind therefore an illness is the person's responsibility
- Depression is a choice
- All mistakes are unconsciously deliberate, therefore "I didn't mean to" is no excuse

Remember that your clients may or may not believe these things, and nothing is guaranteed to upset a client more easily than what they would perceive as inappropriate and "unfair" blame. Eg, avoid telling a depressed client that they can choose to feel better!

The idea of responsibility is crucial in coaching, as the client needs specifically to take responsibility for what is achieved in the process. You need to keep the client accountable, give them the responsibility for sticking to tasks, and then give them credit for achievements. If you take responsibility for their progress, that is inappropriate (sorry!)

However, the coach has significant responsibility to control the process. The client is in control of the content, you are in control of the process. You have a responsibility to behave ethically and to provide a thoroughly professional service to your clients. Part of this is to monitor your own performance.

We advise all coaches to seek professional support and to use checklists to review their own commitment, presence and to look for blind spots.

Case example

Sally ran a successful interior design business, and was wanting to sell her business as a going concern. She had had several potential buyers but all backed out. In discussion with her coach, it transpired that Sally believed that the only reason her business was a success was because the clients felt sorry for her as she is deaf. Her coach was able to challenge this, and Sally realised that she was giving insufficient credit to her staff, and that she did truly believe that another boss would be able to get the same results from them. This is an example of where responsibility issues can interfere with outcome.

The processes that Sally and her coach went through enabled her to pitch her business more accurately, and so get the sale she desired.

Truth

Your client needs to be able to rely on you to be absolutely truthful. You need to be explicit about this, and ensure that they know to expect this.

It is a very unusual situation to be in; not only being allowed to be completely honest, but having to be! And it's rather difficult!

By creating the relationship (as will be described starting on P26) you are creating an environment in which truth is possible. It can, as with responsibility, be easier to raise these issues while the client is in hypnosis. It's also important that your truth encompasses differences in perception and TACT.

Imagine a client who you see face to face is looking to get a new job. When they come to see you, they are wearing odd socks, in need of a shave and have BO. It might be considered truthful to say:

"If you go to an interview like that, you don't stand a chance. You need to get yourself together; you are a mess and you smell"

But this has forgotten perception and tact! Maybe this would be better:

"Do you remember that I promised that I would be truthful with you, and by being so you know that you can trust all the comments I make about you, good or bad? Well, let's think about what an interviewer may be looking for, bearing in mind that initial impressions often (rightly or not) count a lot. Today you are wearing odd socks. Maybe you like to, but if I were an interviewer, I would see that as a sign of being somewhat careless and might wonder whether you would be careless at work. You also haven't shaved, which similarly might be interpreted as not caring. So you might like to think about how you present yourself, looking at it from their point of view. Finally, this is a delicate one, but perhaps I could just say that it might be time for that t-shirt to have a wash......"

Note the "gentle" use of language that would be matched with gentle tones. The coach would also be looking for reactions, verbally or non-verbally to what was being said throughout and adapt as required.

It may be possible to utilise hypnotic tools such as surface structure metaphor for such situations, or to use questioning to allow clients to come to their own conclusions.

Finally, a reminder that "truth" is rarely absolute, so most "truths" would be best couched in terms of opinion to be on the safe side.

Exercise

Over the next week, notice three times when you do NOT tell the truth. What would it have been like to do so? What caused you to lie/omit?

Change

Checklist for change:

1. We all have an innate fear of change: challenge this fear!
2. Change makes you feel good!
3. Change implies choice
4. Change means growing
5. Change means self-evaluation: not relying on the views of others
6. Change means accepting and valuing your feelings as valid
7. Change means learning
8. Change gradually: small, positive steps
9. Keep changing: make it a habit!

Develop a NO LIMITS! Attitude. Then you can

- Change now
- See yourself reaching your goals
- Cope with hurt
- Deal with the unknowns in life
- Have what you want
- Ask for help
- Ask to have your needs met
- Know you are important
- Enjoy life

Here are a few things that you will find yourself saying more often as you choose to change:

Yes	NOT	Yes but...
I did	NOT	I didn't
I can	NOT	I can't
Now	NOT	Later
Sorry	NOT	It's your fault
I will	NOT	I won't
Maybe	NOT	No
I could	NOT	I should

Case example

Rico was a 22 year old draughtsman at a company that employed a coach to work with staff who they thought were underachieving. At his initial interview he stated that he was content in his job, and felt as though he was happy to stay in that role forever.

The coach used time line future pacing in hypnosis, encouraging Rico to dream about how he would like his life to be if there were no restrictions. He saw himself not as a draughtsman, but as an architect, using his creative talents to design state of the art office buildings.

The coach was then able to help Rico to move from an "I can't" attitude, to an "I can", and to see the benefits of change.

At the time of writing, Rico is just completing his degree, undertaken part time with the backing of the company, and is ready to start work, for the same firm, as a junior in their development department.

This change has had significant knock on effects in other areas of his life, and he is now unwilling to settle for less than the best in his personal life too.

Discovering

Setting up the relationship

Introduction

Coaching is a profession which involves interaction with people. Being a coach means adopting a role while your client adopts a corresponding role. Coaches brings aspects of themselves into the role, ie they are real people interacting with other real people.

The paragraph above may appear to be stating the obvious, but this is of crucial importance to the success of your coaching and therefore your success as a Hypnotic Coach.

We believe the relationship that is created between you, the coach, and your client is the most significant factor. Can you think of any profession that involves interaction between people that is not aided by good interpersonal skills? We have all seen examples of those who do not see it as important: the patronising doctor, the authoritarian teacher, the bullying policeman, but what is really needed is CONTACT. Contact between one human being and another. One understanding the other and showing that understanding.

Creating a relationship based on honesty, truth, trust and acceptance is so powerful it almost defies words. But this must be your aim, with each and every client or potential client.

The coach is responsible for building this relationship. By offering this, clients can respond and find themselves in a position where they can change, and change is fundamentally what they come to coaching for.

Exercise

Make a list of your roles (you may have dozens) and next to each role give yourself a rating out of 5 for how well you are in "contact" with the other parties in the relationship. What does this tell you about yourself?

Core conditions

Most counselling and therapy models have the idea of the relationship between client and therapist at their core. The theories are given many names but all stress the need for the client to feel safe; it is this safety which allows exploration and provides a space for experimentation and thence change.

The relationship between coach and client is somewhat different from that between therapist and client, but it is our belief that the importance of the nature of the relationship and the provision of safety cannot be over-emphasised.

The client needs to trust the coach, perhaps more so than even a therapist, as a coach will be giving advice and the client needs to know that the coach has their best interests at heart. This trust can best be developed by creating a relationship based on the Rogerian Core Conditions.

These conditions are often misinterpreted, as they have been adapted by the client-centred counselling theorists to sometimes an extreme stance of a lack of challenge. As a coach, however, challenge is very much a part of your work. But this can be done from the angle of the core conditions.

The core conditions are;

EMPATHY.
UNCONDITIONAL POSITIVE REGARD
CONGRUENCE.

Empathy

"Empathy is the ability to perceive the internal frame of reference of another with accuracy, and with the emotional components and meanings which pertain thereto, as if one were the other person, but without ever losing the 'as if' condition. Thus it means to sense the hurt or the pleasure of another as he senses it, and to perceive the causes thereof as he perceives them, but without ever losing the recognition that it is as if I were hurt or pleased etc. If this 'as if' quality is lost, then the state is one of identification."

Rogers (1959)

OR:

The ability to

- grasp deeply the subjective world of another
- try to be in another's shoes
- understand that their background has caused these ways of being
- recognise that you do not know everything about them

THIS SHOWS:

- understanding
- acceptance
- not being judged

Unconditional Positive Regard

"When the therapist is experiencing a warm, positive and
acceptant attitude toward what *is* in the client, this facilitates
change. It involves the therapist's genuine willingness for the
client to be whatever feeling is going on in him at that
moment, - fear, confusion, pain, pride, anger, hatred, love,
courage, or awe. It means that the therapist cares for the
client, in a non-possessive way. It means that he prizes the
client in a total rather than a conditional way. By this I mean
that he does not simply accept the client when he is
behaving in certain ways, and disapprove of him when he
behaves in other ways. It means an outgoing positive feeling
without reservations, without evaluations. The term we have
come to use for this is unconditional positive regard. Again
research studies show that the more this attitude is
experienced by the therapist, the more likelihood there is
that therapy will be successful."

Rogers

Congruence

"The first element in the creation of the climate has to do with what has variously been called the therapist's *congruence*, realness, authenticity or genuineness. In essence this congruence depends on the therapist's capacities for being properly in touch with the complexity of feelings, thoughts and attitudes which will be flowing through them as they seek to track their client's thoughts and feelings. The more they can do this the more they will be perceived by their clients as people of real flesh and blood who are willing to be seen and known and not as clinical professionals intent on concealing themselves behind a metaphorical white coat. The issue of the therapist's congruence is more complex than might initially appear. Although clients need to experience their therapist's essential humanity and to feel their emotional involvement they certainly do not need to have all the therapist's feelings and thoughts thrust down their throats. Therapists must not only attempt to remain firmly in touch with the flow of their own experience but must also have the discrimination to know how and when to communicate what they are experiencing. It is here that to the objective observer person-centred therapists might well appear to differ widely in style. In my own attempts to be congruent, for example, I find that verbally I often communicate little. I am aware, however, that my bodily posture does convey a deep willingness to be involved with my client and that my eyes are highly expressive of a wide range of feeling - often to the point of tears. It would seem that in my own case there is frequently little need for me to communicate my feelings verbally: I am transparent enough already and I know from experience that my clients are sensitive to this transparency. Another therapist might well behave in a manner far removed from mine but with the same concern to be congruent. Therapists are just as much unique human beings as their clients and the way in which they make their humanity available by following the flow of their own experiencing and communicating it when appropriate will be an expression of their own uniqueness. Whatever the precise form of their behaviour, however, person-centred therapists will be exercising their skill in order to communicate to their clients an attitude expressive of their desire to be deeply and fully involved in the relationship without pretence and without the protection of professional impersonality."

Brian Thorne

Exercise

Over the next few days be aware of when you are really being you and when you are "pretending". If you find that you are being unreal, test out how it would feel to reveal that bit more of yourself.

Achieving the core conditions

To achieve empathy, acceptance, realness and create a safe place for the client, a coach needs:

- An ability to be involved whilst also detached, to be outside as well as inside.
- To have their own feelings/opinions but keep them out of the session.
- To focus on the client, rather than the coach's own needs/views.
- Judge behaviour rather than the person (and refer them on if cannot).
- Show respect at all levels, keeping time, quality of room, giving full attention etc.
- To be aware of own bias, blocks and work with these.
- To be prepared to look at what is raised in themselves by the client.. what do they tell you about your self.. who do they remind you of?
- To be committed to growth and professionalism
- To be open and receptive.
- To use intuition but always check it out.
- To ever over-step empathy by invasion. The client has the choice of how far to let you in.
- To stay congruent: with self (by owning own views and feelings) and with the client (by owning response to their behaviour and not blaming)
- To not collude.
- To use 'responsibility language' ..'I' statements and acknowledgement of choices.
- To maintain own boundaries and empower the client to have their own.
- To explore why the client is behaving/feeling as they do.

In these ways the coach establishes rapport with the client and builds a relationship based on understanding the other person.

The client needs to know that there is nothing that cannot be discussed with the coach. By creating this environment you are enabling the client to feel safe to share and explore anything.

Finally, the client should be encouraged to keep the process "secret"! There is nothing worse than loved ones laughing at your goals, or watching for you to slip up. Goals can be shared when they are reached, and the process shared with the coach.

Further Reading Recommendations:

Person Centred Counselling in Action: Mearns & Thorne
The authors of this course have differing opinions on the
value of person-centred counselling due to very different
experiences of this. However, whatever its value as a therapy
in its own right, this book gives an excellent introduction to
the concepts of creating a therapeutic alliance, which
translates very well to being used in the coach/client
relationship.

The Reality Game: John Rowan
This book is an introduction to humanistic counselling and
once again gives a good insight into the basics of creating
rapport and how this affects the process of change.

Relationship Capital: True Success Through Coaching and
Managing Relationships in Business and Life: Carlos Raimundo

Initial interviews

The initial interview is of great significance for the following reasons:

1. Sets up the relationship, allowing you to demonstrate the core conditions and so start the process of creating rapport.
2. Gives you and the client a chance to get to understand each other and the issues involved.
3. Sets the groundwork for future work.

How you conduct the initial interview will depend on several factors:

1. Your own personality and style of working
2. The client, their reason for seeking coaching and their comfort level
3. Whether you are coaching face to face, by phone of electronically.

For example, if you are experienced in coaching and have a counselling qualification, you are likely to feel more at ease with asking in depth questions early on. Equally, if your client appears timid or in distress, you may keep more distance. If you are face to face you are better able to judge the person's comfort with the questions and so may be able to delve further than by phone, but using the internet, the client may be able to give more detail as they will be able to give more thought to what is said and the "distance" may offer some safety.

The sample interview given below is therefore only a possibility.

Sample Initial questionnaire

Here is a sample intake questionnaire. As stated above, it will not suit every coach or every client, and it can be adapted to your individual preferences and the circumstances in which it is being used. There is another version in "Co-active Coaching" in two parts, on p181 and 184-185.

You may choose to have a more basic form to start with, perhaps to use as part of an initial consultation. If you use a comprehensive form such as this, make sure you get permission for asking in depth questions and explain why before you start.

Name
Date of birth
Place of birth
Nationality

Your mother's name
Her nationality
Her age when you were born

Your father's name
His nationality
His age when you were born

Were your parents married when you were born?
Were they happy together?
Did they stay together?
If not, what happened, when?
Is your mother still alive?
If not, when and how did she die?
How was your relationship with her when you were small?
How has it been since you grew up?

Is your father still alive?
If not, when and how did he die?
How was your relationship with him when you were small?
How has it been since you grew up?

Tell me about your brothers and sisters. Their names, ages, how things were/are between you.

Tell me about any other important relations/others during your childhood.

Tell me about your first love. What happened, how old were you?

Tell me about your current partner (if you have one). Their name, age, how long you've been together, how things are between you.

Tell me about any other significant relationships you've had.

Do you have children? If so, tell me their names, ages, who their other parent is, do they live with you, if not, do you have contact?

Are there other significant people in your life?

Are you happy with your home?
What would you like to improve?

Where or how would you like to live?

When did you leave school?
What qualifications did you get?
How was school?
Did you go to College? If so, what did you study and how was it?

What work do you do?
Do you enjoy this?
Have you done anything else?
Do you wish you could do something different?
Are you happy with the conditions at work (money, hours, people, location)?

What do you do when you are not working?
What excites you?
What interests you?
What bores you?

How is your health?
Do you have, or have you had significant medical conditions that affect your life?
Do you smoke?
Do you drink? If so, how much?
Are you physically active?
Do you eat healthily?
Are you happy with your weight?
Are you happy with your body? If not, what bothers you?

Do you have unfulfilled ambitions?
What would you like to do or be?
What stops you?

Who do you admire? What is it about them?

Who do you dislike? What causes that?

Do you like yourself?

What are the best things about you?
What are the worst?
What would your friends say if they saw those answers?
What would your partner and/or family say?

What prompted you to have life coaching?
What do you wish to achieve?
When do you wish to achieve it by?

Contracting

The contract between client and coach must address the following issues:

- Method of contact (in person/phone/email/IRC)
- Duration of sessions (or amount of contact for email)
- Fees and payment methods
- Confidentiality
- Each person's statement of commitment

Here is an example:

Contract between <Coach's name> and <Client's name>

This contract is for weekly telephone coaching, each session being of 60 minutes duration.

Sessions will continue until either party feels it is time to end. Both commit to giving full explanation for their reason for ending.

All terms and conditions outlined in this contract are liable to annual review.

Fees

My fees are £x per month. If a session is to be cancelled, I require a **FULL** 24 **HOURS NOTICE,** otherwise the client or sponsoring organisation is liable for the full cost of the session. The client is to pay by cheque or standing order, monthly, on receipt of an invoice.

Confidentiality

As a professional coach, I treat all information disclosed to me as confidential. In any matters of concern to me, I consult with my supervisor and, if appropriate, reserve the right to discontinue the coaching relationship and do my best to find an appropriate coach or other professional to refer on to. If I have serious concern about the client's safety or the safety of others, confidentiality can be broken although I will attempt to resolve the issue with the client in the first instance. Confidentiality may also be broken if required by law.

Contact

I do not break into sessions to answer the telephone and there are times when I am not contactable. To allow messages to get through I have a telephone answering machine. I am also available between sessions should a client experience serious difficulties which cannot wait until the next session.

Client's commitment:

As with most things in life, the more you put in, the more you will get out of coaching. I will be asking for personal information, for your feelings, beliefs and innermost thoughts. You are free at all times to decide how much to share and how honest to be, with me and yourself. All I insist on is being treated with respect as a fellow human being.

Coach's undertaking:

I will, at all times, give my best advice, suggestions, information and ideas. I am committed to your best interests, but at no time can I be held liable for the results of any actions you choose to take.

I will continue to work for the benefit of my clients through updating of skills, knowledge and personal growth.

If, for any reason, I become incapable of continuing your sessions, I will give as much notice as possible and refund any fees paid for which no service has been given. In no other circumstances will fees be refundable.

If I feel a tape would be of benefit, and I feel I can provide this, it will be provided free of charge. The services of other professionals may be recommended from time to time.

Signed
Date

Signed
Date

Communication

Deep listening

Listening is at the core of coaching. Without good listening skills your client will not FEEL heard, and this feeling of being heard is vital.

We all know people who appear to listen, but we always know whether this is genuine. So you, as a coach must have, or develop, the skill of listening and showing that you have listened.

NB: listening does NOT mean agreeing. We constantly hear people accusing the government of not listening, but what they really mean is not agreeing. This is different, and luckily it will not matter to your client what you think as it is not your job to make changes to their lives: that is their job!

Below is a basic run through of listening skills that would be covered in any counselling skills course. We would encourage you to practise these as much as you can. They may seem unnatural at first, and it is only by practising that you will discover how effective they can be.

Listening Skills

Paraphrasing

Paraphrasing is stating back to the client the essence of what they have just told you, by picking out the most important elements.

For example

Client: "My boss called me into the office, told me to sit down and just glared at me all the time he was finishing his phone call. I was getting really nervous. Then he just launched into a tirade about how my work wasn't good enough and that if I had to have a sick child then I should make sure there was someone there to look after it as I was letting him down. He went on and on and on. He made me feel really small and I found I couldn't stand up for myself so I just snivelled a sorry and it wouldn't happen again and went into the loo and cried."

Coach: "So, just sitting and waiting started you feeling nervous and then you just felt worse and worse until you couldn't answer back?"

Client: "That's right, I was trampled under foot and I need to stop that happening"

Paraphrasing:

- Demonstrates attention and understanding

- Lets the client know he/she has been heard

- Aids clarity for counsellor and client

- Keeps the encounter focused

- Reassures by validation

- Keeps the flow going

- Gives the client a chance to correct, a feedback for accuracy

- Allows insight and shift of perspective

- Allows for greater self-awareness for the client

- Aids awareness of client's perspective for the counsellor

- Gives space and pace

- Allows counsellor to unburden self of client's problems

- Enables the client to adjust, expand and find what's important

Reflecting Feelings

This skill involves the coach acting as a mirror to the client, but showing the feelings involved rather than the content (or story).

For example:

Client: "I was just so tired that when she started on at me to bath the baby, I just snapped and all my good intentions went out of the window. It didn't help that just then the phone rang and it was my business partner telling me I had to phone an awkward so and so who didn't want to pay his bill. "

Coach: "It sounds as though you felt angry and by being tired you were less able to stop yourself showing these feelings"

Reflecting feelings:

- Brings hidden emotion to the surface

- Gives client 'permission' to have and express feelings

- Acceptance of feelings allows client to accept them too

- Helps the client and counsellor explore what is really there

- Takes the session to a deeper level

- Aids the formation of the therapeutic relationship

- Clarifies, checks and allows correction

- Keeps flow going

- Demonstrates empathy

NOT FOR   passing comment
                  making judgment
                  adding in something of your own

Summarising

Summarising is used to reflect back the salient points of a client's story so that they have a synopsis to take away with them. It can be used intermittently during a session or at the end to summarise the whole thing.

Summarising:

- Underlines the important points, (not all, so acts as a filter.)

- Helps counsellor and client remember what has been said

- Emphasises value of client, acts as further reassurance

- Provides another chance for the client to correct

- Puts the essence of the session into an acceptable form

- Underlines and reinforces paraphrasing

48

- Gives the session a structure

- Gives the client a 'package' to take away

- Acts as a transition, helping the client to recover

- Takes the client from the emotional to the cognitive

- Brings the client back into the world

- Helps to end the session

The Use of Questions

We will talk more of questions later, but initially it is important to become aware of the value of asking questions. You will find that the vast majority of clients are very happy to be asked what may appear at first glance to be rather intrusive questions (in fact you will also find that as you get used to asking questions, so you will do so more in your everyday life: and strangely, it is rare that people object!) .

Questions can be used:

- To help get started

- For elaboration

- To get clearer

- To get to the specifics

- To bring the client to now

- To focus on the client, not others

- To focus on feelings, not facts

- To encourage responsibility

NOT
- for filling in silence
- for own interest
- for making suggestions / possibilities / comment / judgement
- for a conversation

Gestalt use of language

Gestalt uses different rules of communication from everyday conversation, aiming to promote active dialogue and awareness. It is an approach that uses language to

> take responsibility
> be clear
> be in the now
> be direct

Taking responsibility

NOT using	It, You, We, One	which disown and keep the feeling outside
USING	I statements	

Avoid Generalizations

- One does this ....
- We all feel ....
- It's well known that people feel....

CHANGE TO:

- I do
- I feel
- I know that

Change to making direct statements rather than indirect ones

- Instead of not asking directly for what we need we can ask for it clearly.
- Instead of making comments to the air in generalizations, we can tell the person concerned how we really feel.

Claiming/owning choice

- I can't becomes I won't/I choose not to
- I should/I must becomes I prefer to/I choose to.
- I had to becomes I decided to/I choose to.

Past/present as Figure/Ground

Talking about events and feelings as though they are out there in the past avoids uncomfortable emotions. Describing them in the here and now brings us into contact with the feeling.

Acknowledging

Acknowledging leads on from unconditional positive regard in that it is one step beyond. UPR sees the client in a positive light and communicates this, acknowledging is more specific. For example, UPR might be saying to a client who is struggling with a feeling of failure, "I hear you saying that your father would see this as failure, but let's look at how you feel and how what you have experienced will affect you in the future." Acknowledging might be saying "I hear you saying that your father would see this as failure, but I want to say that it seems to me that you have come a long way in the last year when they didn't even want you to stay on for finals. You have a degree now and that is a good thing! So let's look now at how you feel and how what you have experienced will affect you in the future."

For students who come from a counselling background, making positive judgements like this may seem odd (for those who don't this comment may seem odd!), but the coach's primary role is to be the client's number one fan. Positive reinforcement (done congruently) is paramount! If you can't give this to a particular client then they and you are not compatible so refer on.

Acknowledging can be easier for both coach and client, and done more powerfully, using hypnosis.

Exercise

Make a list of 5 friends and write an acknowledgement for each. Would you be able to share this with them? If not, what is stopping you?

Collusion

When you find yourself getting caught up in agreeing with the client, being fascinated by the content and asking questions for you own interest, making comments on the other people and the situation, then you are communicating a judgement and may well be colluding with them. This is different from having positive regard which means communicating your acceptance and valuing of the client without judgement.

In a typical counselling relationship, collusion is comparatively easy to avoid; in coaching it is trickier as one of the coach's main roles is to be the client's biggest fan, motivator and supporter!

So the tricky part is to do this, without colluding for the problems detailed below can still occur.

Examples of collusion:
"That sounds awful for you"
"how upsetting"
"so he made you feel angry"
laughing with them when it wasn't funny
"Oh I know"
"Yes people are so.........."
"So there was nothing you could do about it"
"How uncaring of her"

Why might we do it?
Feeling sympathy, it's easier, because the client is manipulating us, to avoid confrontation, to rescue, for our own needs (eg to be liked, in control), through boredom, through wanting to get results.

When you notice yourself doing this, or feel the impulse to do it then:

- Use empathy as a focus, NOT sympathy, getting into their experience alone, helps keep YOU out of it.

- If the CONTENT is interesting, ask how they are in it or keep paraphrasing. This moves into PROCESS and gets away from your connection to the content.

- Remember you do not know any one else in the story and don't know their experience so don't pass comment on them, reflect back that this is your client's experience of these people/the situation.

- Keep boundaries. You care but are not involved.

Case example

Josephine would, it seemed, constantly pressurise her coach, trying to get him to collude with her "maltreatment" at the tennis club. Everyone would "gang up" on her, or "exclude her on purpose". It was the coach's role to empathise with her feelings, and help her to understand and deal with the issues that arose, but not to agree with her that the others were being "beastly" (as Josephine described it).

This was tricky for the coach as he had been a victim of bullying but, using supervision for support, he was able to keep his own feelings out of the equation. After several weeks of the issue being brought up, and the coach feeling pushed, he decided to raise the issue and Josephine said that she felt that if he didn't agree with her, then he was as bad as the bullies at the club.

The coach suggested that some trance work might be useful to uncover the reasons for Josephine's need, and this revealed a "long forgotten" incident as a child when she had been laughed at for being afraid of a boy in the playground. She had gone to her father for support and he had laughed too.

Josephine was able to recognise that her father's laughter was different from that of her friends at school, and that he was doing his best to support her. This helped her to understand that her interpretation of her coach's response was inappropriate, and this in turn allowed her to analyse more effectively the treatment that she received at the tennis club.

In that situation she had "suffered alone", through fear of what would happen if she asked her husband for support. She then faced this fear, and having enlisted his help, she was able to challenge the two key protagonists who expressed regret at their actions, stating that they hadn't realised what they were doing. Both Josephine and the coach doubted the veracity of this statement, but the result was that things changed very much for the better at the club.

Beliefs

We all have a huge number of beliefs about ourselves and the world. It can be difficult to draw the line between a fact and a belief.

Your clients will be coming to you with their view of the world, which will not be the same as yours.

These beliefs will be underpinning all your work with the client, right from trivial beliefs (eg bacon sandwiches should be cut in squares not triangles), through to beliefs about themselves (eg I am not clever enough to succeed), through to beliefs about other people (eg men are all untrustworthy), through to beliefs about society (eg religion is the source of all the world's problems).

Many of these beliefs are likely to have been swallowed whole from someone else, usually a parent, school or society. In Gestalt terms this process is called introjection.

One of the main areas to work with a client's introjects is on their beliefs about themselves. As children we are all given messages about who and what we are and should be. These messages, to a greater or lesser extent, help to form our sense of self.

We often hear these "messages" repeated by clients. Anytime the client makes an "I am" statement that is negative, look for the introject. Anytime the client uses an "I should" statement, again look for the message that they may have introjected. AND CHALLENGE!

Here are some examples of personal introjects:

- I am untidy however hard I try
- I am never going to amount to much
- I am hopeless at maths
- I am too sensitive

Here are some examples of "shoulds". Be aware of how many of these can get in the way of a client making progress:

- I should change
- I shouldn't feel like this
- It's all my fault
- I should do better
- I should be slimmer/fitter/more like my mother/better
- I shouldn't complain

If you can get the client to acknowledge and accept the reality of where they are and to choose change if required, you are halfway there!

Labels are a special case of limiting beliefs. As soon as a label has stuck, it is difficult to remove. Here are some such labels:

Stupid	Clumsy	Depressed	Careless
Clever	Good girl	Eccentric	Bonkers
Loser	Scruffy	A joke	Rude
Womaniser	Shy	Delicate	Funny
Gregarious	Paranoid	Polite	Geaky

As you can see, some of these may be perceived as positive, but these can be just as limiting as the negative labels.

So, challenge your client's beliefs, gently and carefully, making sure they feel safe as you do so and safe to explore their true feelings and to re-evaluate. A process that lasts a lifetime!

> "I can't believe that" said Alice
> "Can't you?" said the Queen in a pitying tone. "Try again. Draw a long breath and shut your eyes."
> Alice laughed.
> "There's no use trying." She said. "One can't believe impossible things."
> "I daresay you haven't had much practice," said the Queen. "When I was your age, I always did it for half an hour a day. Why sometimes I believed six impossible things before breakfast."
>
> Lewis Carrol: Alice in Wonderland

Here are some typical beliefs that get in the way of progress:

- Putting others first
- Being too old or too young
- Not enough money
- Too many commitments
- Belief in fate
- Following material goals
- Feeling of not being deserving

Exercise

What beliefs do you hold about yourself and the world? Are they yours or introjected? Make lists and challenge yourself!

Case example

This is an interesting example of a very specific belief that a client had been "given", and how it affected his life. At the age of 10 Mike's father had committed suicide. We can all imagine how traumatic that must have been for the lad, and it was made worse because his cousin, who was then 17, and lived with them, told him that "suicide is hereditary". In his vulnerable state, Mike believed what he was told, and developed the idea that "it is only a matter of time....."

He did not self-present for coaching (why would he when there is no point to anything?), but was sent by his boss. The coach uncovered the "hopelessness" easily enough, but it took quite a lot of hypnotic "digging" to discover the underlying belief. This enabled Mike to recognise that his cousin had been wrong, and that he had choices.

This moment was monumental for both Mike and the coach. There were tears on both sides, and the coaching relationship continued until Mike had found success in his career, and had a new wife with a child on the way. At this point, Mike decided to take some time to "consolidate". As he put it, he "needed time to simply enjoy my life".

Values

Values are often looked upon as being very complex. However, values can be best described as what is important to us. In NLP six key areas have been identified. Values relating to career, relationships, family, health and fitness, personal growth and spirituality. Clare Graves identifies three parts of a values level: environmental conditions, values content and the container (our nervous system). Values are more often than not unconscious, and these govern the way we behave. Values also provide motivation to the way we act as well as acting as criteria for judgement of our actions. Values help people to determine good and bad as well as right and wrong.

According to the American sociologist Morris Massey, there are three key phases of development: Imprinting (0-7), Modelling (8-13) and Socialisation (14-21). The first of these, the imprinting phase generally refers to the ages of birth to 7 years of age. Many of the difficulties clients experience in later life can be traced back to this phase. This is also the phase of our lives where our values begin to take root. These values come from parents, significant others, environment, religion, school and significant experiences.

During the modelling phase children begin to model behaviour which will closely be in alignment with the values which were formed in the previous phase of development. Additionally at this stage children will attempt to find people (significant others) whose values fit their own. When I (Shaun) was at this phase, I tried to model John Wayne, because his values were most closely akin to that of my grandfather, who was a significant creator of my early values system.

Finally in the socialisation phase of development the young adult deciphers their social values as well as how they fit into the greater world around them. At this stage and beyond clients are in a position to begin to challenge their values and attempt to find ways to integrate the learnings of life into their value systems.

Very often when working with clients, coaches will need to be able to help clients to determine what is really important and what is only superficially important. In order to ascertain the client's values, the coach asks "what is important about x?" in order to get between say 5 and 8 statements. For example a coach when working with a person regarding their career can elicit the following values:

- Money
- Satisfaction
- Stability
- Prestige
- Vacations
- Socialisation

Once these things are determined it is essential to determine the order of importance of these values. More often than not, the order in which they are given is not the true order of importance. Generally, the client will report what they think they should say first and then what is really important last. Based on this, the list may very well look like this:

- Socialisation
- Vacations
- Satisfaction
- Stability
- Money
- Prestige

This information is obviously relevant in that knowing what is REALLY important as opposed to SUPERFICIALLY important and will really impact on your interventions and make the work you do that much more powerful.

Case example

Patrick was a car mechanic who was really unclear about his future career. He was successful as a mechanic, and 3 years before the coaching work, he opened his own garage which worked exclusively on luxury motor cars. The reason for his coming for coaching was that he had been given the opportunity to expand his business by acquiring an additional garage 30 miles away from his current place of business. When his values were elicited the following were what was important about expansion:

Money
Satisfaction
Stability
Prestige
Success
Opinion of Peers

Upon doing a values hierarchy with him, the actual values
list was

Satisfaction
Stability
Success
Opinion of Peers
Prestige
Money

Based on this elicitation his coach was able to formulate a
hypnotic intervention which focused on his job/work
satisfaction. After 3 sessions he decided he could achieve this
sense of satisfaction without expanding, which was more in
alignment with the importance he placed on spending time
with his young family

Intuition

Intuition is the coach's best friend. You need to learn to trust
it! It may help to think of intuition as simply the power of the
unconscious mind to notice things that you consciously miss.
If you allow the unconscious to communicate these things to
you, then you are intuitive!

A crucial aspect of intuition however is to check it out. NEVER
presume that an intuitive thought is correct. ALWAYS ask (or
keep the thought to yourself for use later!)

Examples of phrases to use:

- I was just wondering whether....
- A thought just popped into my head: can I check it out with you?
- This may be my stuff, but.....
- I don't know why but I just feel a need to ask....

Case example

Brenda was having coaching to help her to find direction in her personal life, while also wanting to maintain her focus on her career as a journalist. Her coach was taking her through a parts integration process as part of her was wanting to move to London (as this would be a "better place to find a man") while part of her wanted to stay in Devon. The process was successful in that both parts were looking for safety, but the coach felt, intuitively that there was something that Brenda was not mentioning. She had the feeling that perhaps there was more to staying put than just her own security. So the coach asked "I am wondering if there is something else that is keeping you here other than the things you have mentioned? Are there perhaps other people involved?

The coach's intuition proved correct: Brenda's aging parents live in Devon and she was concerned that to move would seem as though she was abandoning them. However she had been trying to stop herself thinking of them as they had been less than supportive of her. This process enabled Brenda to look effectively at the issues and to make a rational choice which involved ensuring their security while also making the right choice for her.

Curiosity

We would like to highlight the need for curiosity as a coach. Curiosity has many advantages, but primarily it shows empathy, interest and that you are "there". You will also find it becoming more and more vital as you experience those times when you make a presumption and find you were wrong. For example, one of the authors recently presumed that a client who expressed a feeling of guilt, felt guilty because she was having an affair with a married man, only to discover that the guilt was not related to his status as married but to her need for sex! What the coach should have done was to ask which aspect of the relationship was resulting in the guilt.

Exercise

Allow yourself to be curious at least five times in the next 24 hours. Ask curious questions of anyone.... Friends, family or even strangers. Dig deeper for information on someone you see on the news, or just question a belief that you or someone else expresses. Ask lots of hows, whys (being careful not to include a judgement) and whens! Have fun!

Further Reading Recommendations:

Wordweaving Vol 1: Trevor Silvester
Trevor (a friend and colleague of the authors) has written this excellent book on the use of language which covers Beliefs and Values in depth.

Changing Belief Systems with NLP: Robert Dilts

Applications of NLP: Robert Dilts

Planning and Doing

Interventions

Interventions are deliberate, conscious acts that facilitate change in performance and are solutions to gaps. Not all interventions will be applicable for a certain type of client, but they are all possible tools in your tool box. Just as a plumber may have a hammer in the tool box and not use it to fix a broken tap, so you may have tools that you rarely use.

Practical guidelines for interventions:

- Consider interventions based on what your client (and not YOU wish to achieve).
- Remain focused on the solution of a problem rather than on a specific intervention. Eg you may have just learnt a new technique, but trying to fit it to your client is inappropriate
- An intervention applied to one setting may not work in another setting.
- Think outside the box, considering less frequently used interventions: both hypnotic and non-hypnotic.
- Evaluate interventions on an ongoing basis to determine their appropriateness and effectiveness.

Elements of successful interventions:

- Choice of intervention should be based on a comprehensive understanding of the situation.
- Interventions should be carefully targeted. Target the right people, the right setting, the right time.
- The intervention must be acceptable to the client.

- If the client is part of a team then the interventions should be designed to fit with the aims of that team. It may be that other members of the team can contribute to the effectiveness of the intervention.
- Interventions should be cost-sensitive. Most of the interventions that we discuss do not necessarily cost anything, but they might! This could be a factor.
- Interventions should be sufficiently powerful. Consider long-term verses short-term effectiveness. Use multiple strategies to effect change.
- Interventions should be sustainable. For example suggesting to a client who needs to lose weight that they will never eat chocolate ever again may be just TOO much!

Some basic techniques to use in coaching:

- In coaching there is usually little attempt to understand the cause of a problem: always start from where the client is now. However, if the client wants to understand the cause, then hypnotic techniques can be utilised, but always keep the focus on how that information will be used to help the client move on. Also, at times, the past interferes and needs to be dealt with (whether the client is initially keen to do so or not!)

> ### Case example
>
> Mohammed is having coaching to help him to set up his own coaching practice. He is having problems with the marketing tasks that the coach sets him. However the coach phrases his suggestions, Mohammed always comes back with some feeble (and he agrees that they are feeble) excuses as to why he has not acted.
>
> His coach respectfully suggests that perhaps they need to discover why Mohammed is avoiding taking this action. He agrees and so they look back and discover that he set up a pattern of avoidance at school when given homework. This originated when, having been quite successful at school, he found A Levels harder and in order to avoid failure, he simply chose not to bother.
>
> Mohammed and his coach were able to determine the risks of "failure" in terms of his marketing and he was therefore able to put aside this old pattern, and, as he put it "go for it

all guns blazing". He did so, and while he has not yet made the success of his business that he would like, he is getting there, and he has had no problem with the marketing that hasn't worked: he has simply learned from it.

- Find out where the client wants to get to and find the quickest way there.

Case example

Tia, who has been having coaching through her employer, has been looking for a partner for several years. She is 35 and wants to have children, but only with a permanent partner. In discussions with her coach it becomes clear (to the coach!) that she has been going about this in an ineffective way. She has been going out three times a week to pubs and clubs, but the majority of the clientele are much younger, and not interested in what she is interested in.

Tia's coach helped her to see that just as if she was marketing a product, she would need to target her advertising, she needs to be in an environment where there is a realistic chance of meeting the right person. After much discussion as to how to do this, Tia decided to advertise in the personal section of the Independent, and has had several dates with men who are a lot closer to her ideal. She is hopeful that this "direct route" will enable her to fulfil her goal.

- Discover what already works and encourage more of it.

Case example

Ron is very organised at work. He is noted in his company for his clear thinking, logical analysis and neat presentation. However at home, he was untidy and drove his wife nuts by his mess. His coach was able to help him see that he could utilise the skills he uses at work, at home. All it took was a choice, and both Ron and Mrs Ron were much happier!

- Sometimes only a tiny change can start a chain reaction leading to resolving a problem.

Case example

Pauline's marriage was going through a bad patch. She felt she wanted to leave, but through hypnotic age progression she realised that the marriage was worth saving. She told her husband that evening, for the first time in three years, that she loved him and they haven't looked back since.

- Focus on the skills, resources and strengths of the client.

Case example

Isa had ambitions to be an author but he was dyslexic. He had always felt that this problem would prevent him achieving. His coach used hypnosis to help him see that he had all the resources that he needed: he had the imagination, the use of language and the time and organisational abilities. The only bit missing was the ability to put his thoughts down on paper more effectively.

Together they investigated and found a local student who was delighted to be able to transcribe audio recordings which Isa dictated on a Dictaphone. Isa was able to pay the student a reasonable hourly rate, so both were happy!

Isa's first novel is in press as this is being written.

- Avoid connecting the problem to the client. This will free them to talk about it.

Case example

Rita was experiencing problems at work which she would not discuss in her coaching sessions. She said that it had to do with her disability but would say no more. Her coach did not press but instead asked her to consider how she would coach another person who was in a similar situation to herself. This enabled Rita to gain understanding about the reactions of other people to her situation, and after some time of looking at the situation this way round, she was able to then look at her own position and her feelings about it.

- Use scaling: on a scale of 1 to 10, where...

Case example

Calum is a golfer who has set a goal of a handicap of single figures by the end of the year. His coach is working with him to help his mental game and to keep his focus and motivation going. However it has proved difficult to understand where Calum "is" at any given time. It may be that he reports a score of 89, but how "good" this is he couldn't determine. This was until he thought of using scales. He now asks Calum how well he feels he played on a scale of 1 to 10, and also how easy the course was, how he felt mentally and how he felt physically.

The coach can also use scaling to see how effective Calum found a particular intervention (for example, in their last session they did some submodalities work on the fear of bunker shots, which Calum rated as 6 out of 10 in terms of helpfulness).

- Can bring others into the scaling. Eg, on a scale of 1 to 10, where would x think you were? What would she/he think you need to get to 10?

Case example

Hilary owns a small hotel which she runs almost single handed. She suffers from low self-esteem and has found it

---

difficult to be sure that decisions that she is making on everything from pricing to new décor are the best ones.

She was very close to the owner (Mrs M.) of a hotel at which she worked as a young woman, and her coach has helped her using scaling by asking how she would rate Hilary's choices. Mrs M. consistently rates Hilary higher than Hilary herself which is giving the coach lots to play with!

- Get the client to write down a number of choices (eg 10 things that could get you more money), then narrow it down. Always ask for a higher number of choices than you think is possible or they will limit themselves!

Case example

Nick wanted to change career and to do something more fulfilling than he was finding his role as a maths teacher. He liked the subject but found keeping discipline in the classroom a problem and this was causing him to feel stressed and was damaging his health.

His coach suggested that he write a list of 50 possible careers that he could take up. Nick's first reaction was that this was ridiculous, but he had a go. He came up with 40, and it was the 35th that gave him the clue that he had been waiting for.

He is now a senior statistician for the local football club, his love of maths and sport morphed together perfectly for his new career. He had felt as if he were stuck in his previous career, but through the elicitation of options run through in his coaching session with additional ego strengthening with hypnosis he is now in a far more fulfilling role.

Some basic questions to ask:

1. How will you know at the end of the session that it was worthwhile having the session today?
2. What makes you set the goal of earning £1 million rather than £2 million
3. How will you know when things are good enough for you to stop coaching?
4. What else should I have asked you?
5. Tell me about the times when it doesn't happen / happens less.
4. When does it bother you least?
5. What is different about those times?
6. If you were to employ someone else to do what you are doing how would you tell them to do it?
7. You report being at 3 on a scale of 1 to 10. What is different that means you are at 3 not 1?
8. How much better would it be to be at 4?
9. How will life look when you are at 10?
10. What are you doing to stop things getting worse?

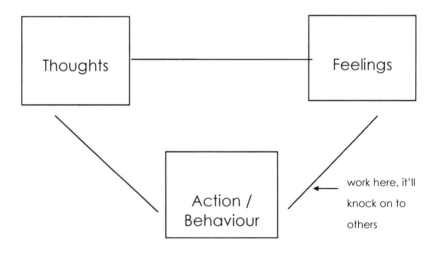

Goal setting

A statement of the obvious:

In order to get what you want, you must know what you want

Ok, so it's not always true: I didn't know I wanted a digital camera until I won one in a competition, but conversely, I would never have got to the position of writing this book if I hadn't known that I wanted to!

A client will often have only a vague idea of what they want and need. Their ideas may be abstract, precise or anywhere in between. They are unlikely to come to you saying "I want to buy a Porsche in 6 months time". More likely they will say "I don't feel I have any status".

So the process is to get the client to the specifics, and then to find routes to achieve the aims.

The Process:

Start from where the client is now.

Look at
- Needs
- Wants
- Desires
- Ambitions   (see p85 for the differences)

You are likely to start with high level abstractions:
- Happiness
- Fulfilment
- Success
- Freedom
- Wealth

As a coach it is part of your role to ensure that your client doesn't limit their choices inappropriately. To this end, we suggest that you encourage your client to "think big". The easiest and most effective way to do this is by a visit (or more than one visit) to the future using hypnosis.

We preframe this with our clients by asking them if they believe that time travel is possible. They almost invariably say no, at which point we tell them that it is possible and always has been: travel to our own past is called remembering, to the wider past is history. Travel to the future is called imagination.

If they are the sort of client who doubts their ability to imagine we can "go to the past" and bring it forward from their childhood. We haven't found a client yet who didn't imagine as a child, but often the ability is "forgotten". The process then is to use a time line to travel forward and to observe their future. We suggest to them that they hover above the line, just as if a car on a motorway, from where you can see a certain way forward and a certain way back, turned magically into a helicopter.

Using this analogy they can move forward (or back) and observe. We encourage them to see all the wonderful things that could be in their future, without any limits; how things could be if anything was possible and if there were no such things as fear and failure, and resources were unlimited.

This gives clients an idea of what they really would like to achieve. Sometimes these desires would not fit in with their lives as they are, but even so the coach can help them to discover what it is about that desire that is appealing and so they can find a way to get that need filled in a congruent way. For example, if a client said that she saw herself, one year from now, running a bar in the Maldives, when currently she is six months pregnant with a two year old, a highly paid job and a huge mortgage, it MAY be that this goal would not fit! However, if she determines that the appeal of this dream is the freedom from drudgery and the sunshine, it may be that the coach can help her to find these things (at least some of the time) in a way that does fit with her circumstances.

From these "impossible dreams", we can begin to set intermediate goals and to find the steps that are needed in order to be able to reach them. Remember a goal is just a starting point. Most goals need action, and sometimes lots of it to reach.

Sometimes we need to encourage the client to get to specifics from their abstract ideas. For example:

Coach: What do you want?
Client: Freedom
Coach: What would you need in order to have freedom, specifically?
Client: Money
Coach: How much money?
Client: Enough money to do what I want
Coach: What specifically?
Client: Provide the family with 'little extras'
Coach: Specifically?
Client: Holidays and a Jacuzzi
Coach: How much do you need, per year to do this?
Client: An extra £8,000

So now we know what the client wants, specifically, and we can move on to look at how and to break this down into small measurable steps and actions to take to move in this direction.

Let's continue the example, and presume the client is a freelance journalist who works mainly for local newspapers and small-scale magazines.

Coach: To get extra income, this could be from your main occupation or from a new source. Which shall we focus on to start with?
Client: My work: journalism
Coach: So you could get more assignments or maximising the income from a piece of work. Which shall we look at first?
Client: Maximising a piece.
Coach: OK. I presume that ethically, you can only sell one piece to only one publication, unless they agree for it to be sold elsewhere?
Client: Yes. Which seems such a waste when I've written a really good piece and only a few people read it.
Coach: But presumably the Exeter local paper wouldn't mind if the article was also put in the Glasgow one? And the Times wouldn't mind if it was printed in the New York Times?
Client: Guess not, but how would I do that?
Coach: Between now and the next session, how would it be to discuss this with other journalists, your professional organisation, editors?
Client: I could do that! I could check the library and bookshops too to see if there are any ideas there!
Coach: Great! And how about also working out how many extra 'resales' you need to sell in order to reach the £8000 a year target?

The goals that a client is specifically working towards should be:

- small rather than large
- concrete, specific, behavioural
- the start of something, not the end
- positive indicators of success, not the absence of problems
- realistic and achievable
- realistically achievable: break them down to short timescales (eg two weeks)
- involve work, as perceived by the client and/or family

When the goals have been set it is vital they should be written down! Drawing can also help, as can creating scrapbooks. But however they are put onto paper they must then be used, not just hidden in a draw.

Goals should be reviewed daily, without fail!

Case example

The coach took Shelly through the exercise in looking at the future as described above. She was at that time a self-employed accountant with a small practice, two children of 6 and 8 and had been married to Geoff for 10 years., She described her marriage as "ok". One year from now Shelly saw herself in very similar circumstances to the present day, except that she was enjoying her time with her family more. She specifically saw herself eating dinner at the table with Geoff and her daughters which was something they never did.

At the three year point she saw her family in a different house. It was older and bigger and she saw herself painting an office for herself (at the time she worked from a rented office). She looked at her bank statement and saw a healthy figure.

At the ten year point she saw herself with Geoff on a tropical beach. The girls were not there. She said that the older one (who would now be 18) was in her first term at University and the younger one was staying with friends. As she lay there on the beach she stated that she was looking forward to returning to work. She now ran an exclusive accountancy practice for successful business women only. She found this very fulfilling.

These "dreams" enabled Shelley to set goals that were intermediate steps en route to fulfilment of these ideals. And immediately the family all started to eat together!

Needs, wants, desires and ambitions

As mentioned on p79, we need to know what a client needs, wants, desires and has ambitions to achieve. So what are the differences between these words? To a great extent it is a personal opinion. For example one person may say they NEED to be sexually desirable, whereas another may say they simply WANT to be (and for others it may not be relevant at all).

Perhaps needs and wants can be seen on a continuum; with a need being a more pressing requirement than a want. There are certain things that simply are needed in life, eg food, water, air, shelter, and others that are clearly "wants", eg a Ferrari rather than a Ford. A desire may be seen as a more intense "want", and is often not something that is seen as being as achievable as a "want". The word "desire" is also often used to describe something that we think we shouldn't have.

Both "want" and "desire" can be in contrast to "need" e.g. an obese person wants or desires a hamburger and chips but does not need them - indeed needs not to have them. Nevertheless, etymologically, 'want' is closer to 'need'.
To want for food is simply to need it in a sense in which to desire it is not. " What do we want - work! When do we want it - now! " : this means want and need. And when Jane Austen wrote of a rich man in want of a wife she meant that he needed one whether he realised it or not.

'Desire' can be more aspirational and longer term - eg. Stephen Gerrard might say: "I want England to win the World Cup but I desire to be a successful footballer."

An ambition is usually some way in the future, and may or may not be perceived as achievable. It is also the only one of these words that is usually about the self. We can want, need or desire things predominantly involving others, but ambitions are usually owned.   The exception is that one can be ambitious for one's children or partner, but it doesn't really work for anyone "less close". Using football again, anyone can say they "want" England to win (unless they are Scottish in which case I believe that statement would result in banishment), but unless a person is involved in the outcome, they cannot say that it is their ambition.

Let's look at some examples of statements that clients may say:

- "I need a bar of chocolate at 3pm every day". This may be perceived as a need, based on a habit, but rationally it is illogical. It cannot be a need, but it may also not be a "want". The client may want to stop this need.
- "I need to make an extra £5000 a year to meet my bill now that the new baby is here". The correct statement here would be that he needs a way to break even (or better). Making an extra £5000 is just one way to meet the real need.
- "I want to work fewer hours; I am close to burn-out". Perhaps this client is really saying "I need to find a way to avoid burn-out"
- "I want to get this promotion". The crucial element here is how much does she want this? Is it a vague want or more of a real desire? What about it does she want?
- "I have always desired beautiful women". This example of the use of the word "desire" may (or may not) suggest something that has the "shouldn't" attached, or perhaps something that is problematic.
- "It is my ambition to build a see-through dam". This was an ambition stated by a student of Civil Engineering. He had no idea how this could be achieved (and his coach couldn't help him on that one!), so it was very much in the future, and little more than a dream.

- "My ambition is to get my handicap down to single figures this year". This use is more akin to a want or desire, and was in this case clearly achievable (he was then on 12). However the use of the word shows a determination that the use of the word "want" may not have

It is worth noting that tone is very important when determining the exact meaning of what you client says in this context. The tone will show where on a continuum of passion, commitment and determination they are: but sometimes this can be used as a form of subtle deception, so beware!

Abraham Maslow developed a Hierarchy of Needs. His idea was that the lower levels of the pyramid needed to be fulfilled before a person would be concerned with the higher levels. However, we see this as a useful guide only. People vary on what is important, and, for example there will be people who strive for creativity before they concern themselves with mastery.

Also, a temporary problem "lower down", would not necessarily stop a person pursuing the higher needs. See next page for a diagram of the Hierarchy.

Maslow's Hierarchy of Needs

Types of Goals

The basic motivations in life are avoidance of pain and pursuit of pleasure. All goals can be chunked up to this ultimately. But motivation also needs energy and the energy to take action needs to be stronger than the energy required to stay still!

The coach is in a unique position to use this rule. A client will often find that it is easier to take action, than to defend their reasons for not doing to their coach!

Away from   Means
Towards   Ends

Eg:

Away from/Means:	to not quarrel with my spouse
Away from/Ends	to avoid dying from heart disease
Towards/Means	to get a sun tan
Towards/Ends	to feel happy

SMART

Goals (the smaller ones we've chunked down to) should embody the SMART acronym:

Specific
Measurable
Adjustable
Realistic
Time-oriented

Achieving outcomes

This process can be used to ensure that goals are achievable and to re-verify from time to time that the client remains on track.

Keys to an achievable outcome

Begin by asking yourself: "How is it possible that I (they) don't have it now?"

1. **Stated in the positive.**
    What specifically do you want?

2. **Specify present situation.**
    Where are you now?   (Associated)

3. **Specify outcome.**
    What will you see, hear, feel, etc., when you have it?
    - As if now.
    - Make compelling
    - Insert in future. Be sure future picture is dissociated.

4. **Specify evidence procedure.**
    How will you know when you have it?

5. **Is it congruently desirable?**
    What will this outcome get for you or allow you to do?

6. **Is it self-initiated and self-maintained?**
    Is it only for you?

7. **Is it appropriately contextualized?**
    Where, when, how, and with whom do you want it?

8. **What resources are needed?**
    What do you have now, and what do you need to get your outcome?
    - Have you ever had or done this before?
    - Do you know anyone who has?
    - Can you act as if you have it?

90

9.   **Is it ecological?**
- For what purpose do you want this?
- What will you gain or lose if you have it?
- What will happen if you get it?
- What won't happen if you get it?
- What will happen if you don't get it?
- What won't happen if you don't get it?

Motivation

What is motivation?

There are many theories of motivation, and we have utilised the ones that we believe are the most useful for our work as Hypnotherapists and Hypnotic Coaches in our book Motivational Hypnotism. Here we will highlight a few key ideas, but if this is an area that particularly interests you (and it should as motivating your clients is a key part of the role of a coach, you may like to consider adding Motivational Hypnotism to your repertoire).

Motivation is about why we do things, what our incentives are, what drives us. We are motivated to act when that action fulfils a need, or moves us in the direction of fulfilling a need. Without this, there is little chance of action.

Let's look at some specific examples of needs motivating action:

- A woman who needs to be accepted may be motivated to do everything for everybody
- A man who needs to be respected may be motivated to work long hours to earn enough to buy a nice car
- A teenager who needs to feel they are one of the crowd may be motivated to smoke
- A woman who needs to prove herself to her father may be motivated to get a PhD
- A man who needs to feel better about himself may choose to bully his employees

Motivation is about:

- Direction: towards the positive or away from the negative

- Persistence: sticking to a task

- Continuing motivation: long term motivation

- Intensity: strength of the desire for change

All of these can be ascertained by the coach, and maximised using hypnotic interventions.

Case example

Fritz was having coaching to help him achieve his goal of becoming a consultant gerontologist. He had set this goal as a teenager as a promise to his dying grandfather whom he adored. At the age of 32, he was close to his achievement and did actually really enjoy the work. The problem was the last step to the role of consultant which was not as appealing as his current role. However he was determined.

Fritz's motivation was towards the pleasure of being able to say that he had done what would have pleased his grandfather and away from his perceived pain of "letting him down". The coach broached the subject of the legitimacy of these beliefs but Fritz was already well aware of this and was choosing to stick to his original decision. His persistence had got him as far as he had got: he described himself as "not as naturally gifted as most of his colleagues at med school", and his continuing motivation never wavered. The intensity of his desire was always high, as long as he thought about it! This was the key: he needed his coach to keep his focus. He was so busy at work that it was too easy to forget all about the ambition amidst the hectic environment of the hospital.

Locus of control

The control theories look at whether the person feels they can control their behaviour and/or the outcome of that behaviour.

Locus of Control is the term used to describe a tendency to presume control to be internal to the self or external. Eg "I determine my results" or "it's all down to fate"

Both the client's general tendency and how they feel about the specific issue are important.

Case example

Isobel's goal was to lose 2 stone within three months, ready for her wedding. She expressed a huge amount of motivation, not least that she had already bought her dress so she "had" to lose the weight or she would not only "feel awful" walking down the aisle but also be out of pocket by a considerable amount of money!

One might think that this would be enough, but no! She was finding that she wasn't making any changes to her behaviours despite hypnotic interventions. The problem turned out to be connected to locus of control. Isobel did not believe that she was able to control her behaviours, and what's more she didn't trust that eating the right things and exercising more would result in the weight loss she wanted.

This realisation enabled the coach to adapt his interventions to help her take control and believe in her abilities. She almost met her goal: she lost 20lbs and with the extra toning from the exercise she got into her dress and felt brilliant as she walked down the aisle!

Intrinsic and extrinsic motivation

Intrinsic motivation is being motivated by the process itself, typically for interest, challenge or enjoyment.

There are also three needs that may be met by intrinsic motivation:

- relatedness
- competence
- autonomy

The more the coach can help a client to be intrinsically motivated by either the goal and/or the behaviours necessary to reach the goal, the more likely the client is to be successful.

Case example

Steven has set himself the goal of running the London marathon next year. He has worked with his coach to maximise his enjoyment of his training, building in weekly challenges and adding interest by changing his training run routes.

He has started to run with a friend, which is helping with his feeling of relatedness (he had been feeling a little isolated). Meeting his challenges (when he does) helps him feel competent and he is making his own choice to do this so knows he is autonomous.

The coach has also used future pacing to help Steven see how meeting the goal (running and completing the marathon) will also be enjoyable, challenging, interesting and help him to meet these needs.

Extrinsic motivation is being motivated by factors outside the process itself, such as rewards, approval or pressure.

It can be delineated into a continuum of self-determination:

- External: I must
- Introjected: I should
- Identified: I want to
- Integrated: It is important to me

The more the coach can help the client to move towards the lower portions of this continuum the better. However, extrinsic motivation should be used with caution. Sometimes these things backfire, but sometimes they are really useful. An example might be of someone who is taking a course. Talking to them about the certificate they get at the end of the course MAY help their motivation to do the work (one of the authors (not Fiona) is known to have taken courses because the certificate was pretty), but may not be motivating. If the certificate means nothing, then this would "jar" and the client may find it hard to accept other ideas that are offered.

Also, if a person gets used to getting rewards for certain behaviours, and then the rewards cease, it may be that they will discontinue the behaviour even if it is beneficial in other ways.

Case example

Val wanted to quit smoking as part of her overall goal of regaining her health and fitness. However, she felt that this was something that she MUST do. She didn't want to, and said to her coach that she really enjoyed smoking and would feel deprived when she had stopped. Her coach helped her to realise that the overall goal was important and that smoking would significantly get in the way of her overall achievement if she carried on. She also helped Val to recognise that she didn't actually enjoy smoking itself, but rather she enjoyed what it brought: namely time to herself, relaxation and a sense of doing what she wanted rather than what she was supposed to be doing.

With this realisation she was able to get these needs met more appropriately. The coach also worked with Val on the issues of approval (which originally Val specifically didn't want), and pressure which had been a de-motivator.

Attributions

Clients may attribute success or failure to ability, effort, task difficulty or luck. The coach can ascertain their patterns of attribution and may well find areas which can be utilised for the specific goals the client is working on, or maybe identify patterns that are less than helpful.

Attributions can be internal or external, stable or unstable. Let's look at an example: taking a maths test. A client may say:

- "I passed this exam because I was lucky" (success: external)
- "I failed this exam because I didn't work hard enough" (failure: internal)
- "I passed this exam because I am good at maths" (success: internal)

- "I failed this exam because it was too hard" (failure: external)

It is important to look for reality as well as the patterns. It could be that any of these statements are "true", but uncharacteristic. For example the second client may have passed every other test because "he was good at maths" but just had a hiccup here.

Case example

Andy was working towards his first million selling electronic components. He had a good lifestyle and had employed a coach to help him to maximise the 20 hours per week that he wanted to work. His philosophy was that there was no point in having lots of money without time to enjoy it. He attributed his success at work to his natural ability and hard work (internal attributions). However, the coach, being holistic, felt that Andy needed to look at every aspect of his life, and found that the main problem was that he wasn't enjoying his time off as he was alone, and lonely.

The coach gently asked how it was that Andy had no partner, and Andy attributed it to the fact that he is a geek and has not tried to change in order to be attractive to women (internal attributions again). It seemed that Andy takes responsibility for everything, which can be helpful, sometimes not.

In this instance, Andy was able to realise that he could make some differences, and make some progress towards getting a partner. He employed what he called a "style guru", had his hair styled, bought a whole new wardrobe, a new car (previously he had a specialist car that cost a fortune but looked "weird"). He also employed a publicist who ensured that he was written up in his local paper (as well as national specialist media). He then found a friend to accompany him and set out to "hit the clubs". His strategy was so successful he decided that he wasn't any longer looking for one woman but would "play the field" for a while.

Andy's coach has since been watching his career, and life, with interest. Perhaps one day he will return!

Dweck's theory

Carole Dweck has developed a theory concerning people's beliefs about ability. She states that people tend either to have an

> entity view: belief that attributes (eg ability) are
> relatively fixed

or an

> incremental view: belief that attributes are open
> to development

it is our opinion that most people have a variation in their beliefs. For example a person may believe that if they practice consistently they can improve their tennis, but not their maths.

It is very useful information to know about your client!

Stages of change

Prochaska and Di Clemente have developed a theory on how change happens. The coach can share this theory with the client to help them progress. The stages are:

- Precontemplation
- Contemplation
- Preparation
- Action
- Maintenance

Let's look at an example of a person quitting smoking. The precontemplation stage is the time before they have even begun to think about quitting. They then begin to think that maybe it is time to stop and enter the contemplation stage. Perhaps they are beginning to be aware of breathing problems, or others are nagging them to stop, or they are feeling ostracised in company.

The next step is for them to think about how to stop. This is the preparation stage. They may discuss their decision with friends and family and seek information about alternative methods, including perhaps hypnosis, acupuncture, NRT and "cold turkey". If they decide on a particular route they may then seek the details, perhaps searching the web for local hypnotherapists.

The action stage is, of course, when they stop. In this example the action takes moments. One moment they are a smoker, the next a non-smoker. The process could be lengthened by cutting-down over a period of time, but the crucial stage for ex-smokers is the maintenance stage.

As a hypnotic coach your clients will often be at a different stage than your usual hypnotherapy clients. Anyone going for hypnotherapy is likely to be at "action", or perhaps "preparation". Coaching clients could be anywhere, including precontemplation as your work will involve helping them to decide on the changes that they want to make and it will often be the case that they have not even considered a change that becomes apparent during the coaching process.

You then have a unique opportunity to use your coaching and hypnotic skills with each stage. This can maximise the effectiveness of each, resulting in easy (or easier!) change and long-lasting effects.

Case example

Pearl was having coaching simply because she felt dissatisfied with life. Various tools were utilised, incuding some in hypnosis which led Pearl to realise that she needed to move out of her parents' house and to get a place of her own. She was 22 and had always thought that she wouldn't leave home until she married (there was no prospect of that at that time). (End of the precontemplation stage).

Her coach helped her, once the decision was made, to feel strong enough to go through with it, using ego-strengthening and helping her to find her own resources. Pearl also spent some time in coaching looking objectively at her options, practically, financially and emotionally. (Contemplation).

Pearl decided to move into a small flat much nearer to her work than her parents' house. As it was in the inner city it was cheap (comparatively) and she would save time and money on travel. She arranged a mortgage and was continually supported by her coach, finding this environment useful to explore her fears as well as look at the potential benefits. At other times she would find it too easy to get caught up either in the excitement (when she would forget the risks) or the fear (when she would forget the reasons for the move). (Preparation).

On her 23rd birthday, Pearl moved into her flat. (Action). She loved it, felt happy to have made an autonomous choice, and felt freed to concentrate on fulfilling her other goals. In this case "maintenance" was not a factor: she was never going back, except to visit of course!

Tasking

Tasking is one of the most crucial aspects of the coaching relationship. It is one of the fundamental ways of motivating your clients. As long as you ensure they do not see this as being like "homework" (unless of course they liked homework!), you will find that being required to complete tasks, which are designed completely for their benefit (this fact must be 100% clear), will be appreciated.

It is important that tasking is built into the understanding of the relationship, but you, as coach need to be aware that you are "requesting" your client to do things, but you cannot make them! They always have a choice. As choice is one of the primary things that you are encouraging all your clients to accept as a basic premise in life, this can work to your advantage!

Clients have the option of saying "yes", "no", "I'll think about it" or making a counter offer. It can be a good idea to set up the thought of counter offers at the contracting stage, to avoid the "no". However, a "no" can open up an interesting line of discussion. Why are they saying no? Some sort of resistance must be going on, but what does it mean?

When the client has agreed to a task in general, let's say to call two firms each day to enquire about job vacancies, the task then needs to be pinned down. Here are the standard questions to ask, which can be varied according to the circumstances:

1. What will you do?
2. When will you do it?
3. How will I know?

In the above example, it would be more appropriate to ask "How are you going to choose the firms to call?" rather than question one as the "what" was already clear.

SMART

Tasks should embody the SMART acronym (just as goals):

> Specific
> Measurable
> Adjustable
> Realistic
> Time-oriented

A specific way to do this is to encourage them to set their own consequence system in place. Consequences are to be positive for achievement, and negative for the opposite. In our example, the client may decide to put £5 toward a new dress for every call she makes, and to give £5 to charity for every call she misses. Amounts will obviously vary according to the person's circumstances, and consequences do not need to involve money.

Positive thinking

"With a positive mental attitude you cannot fail to succeed. With a negative mental attitude you cannot fail to fail."

But then:

"There is no such thing as failure: only feedback!"

(Clearly both these quotes are technically false, but they are interesting ideas to contemplate)

Everything is an outcome of an action. Depending on your perception of the outcome, actions can be repeated/avoided/adapted to produce the same or different outcomes.

Set backs can be considered as opportunities for learning, improving and testing one's resolve.

Positive thinking is vital to achieve success, fulfilment and to reach your goals. However, positive thinking needs to be combined with positive action. Making positive affirmations every day is fine, but on its own will do little.

The bottle may be perceived as half full or half empty, but this doesn't change reality. In fact too much positive thinking can result in a client falling short of reaching their potential. If they are content with a half full bottle, what's to motivate them to fill it?

Here's an example of an intervention

Coach: How are you today?

Client: Great: I just scored 55% in my mock exams which is fine: that is enough to pass and then I can stay on for next year. I am feeling very positive about my work.

Coach: What would happen if you got 70% at the end of this year instead?

Client: Well, then I would have a greater cushion for next year when I take my finals as I'd have already got a first in this year's 25%.

Coach: So would that be worth aiming for?

Client;   I can try

Coach: How would it be to consider what you need to do and then just do it, rather than trying?

Client: Seems like a plan: I will feel better about what I am doing, and I'm almost certain to do better than I would have!

Exercise

Think of someone you know (not you, surely?) who has a negative attitude. Write down a few things you have heard them say, and then rephrase them in a positive light. How did you feel when writing the negative and the positive?

Feedback

One of the most powerful coaching skills is the ability to give constructive feedback, both positive and negative. Feedback is direct, clear and, most important, without judgement. Communication *with* judgement is praise or criticism.

4 elements for giving constructive feedback:

1. Content -- *what* you say.
    Identify the issue or behavior in your first sentence. Provide the specifics or evidence. Begin the statement with an "I" message, such as "I have noticed" or "I have observed."

2. Manner -- *how* you say it.
    Be direct and clear without hesitation.
    Avoid giving "mixed" or "yes, but" messages.
    State observations, not interpretations.
    Give feedback face-to-face.

3. Timing -- *when* to give feedback.
    Feedback is meant to be given as close as possible to when the event occurred. However, when giving negative feedback, take the time, if necessary, to "cool off" and get clear on your thoughts.

4. Frequency -- *how often* to give feedback.
    On an ongoing basis! Feedback may occur at any time and with any frequency, depending on the purpose of the feedback. When giving negative feedback, allow time for the person to digest what was said, to paraphrase back to you, and time to have a dialog about the concern.

Championing

We highlight this skill here due to its critical importance for the coaching relationship. We have already stated that a coach's job is to be the client's number one fan, and championing is a way to demonstrate this and to support the client in their endeavours.

This is where a professional coach is most like a sports coach. Imagine a football coach encouraging his players at half time, or a Davis Cup coach during the deciding rubber, or a Ryder Cup captain during the final round.

This action can even be likened to fans supporting their team: "Come on you Spurs".

How wonderful it will be for your clients to have someone supporting the like this! However, this may feel unnatural, both to you and them: so practise!

Exercise

Make a list of 10 friends, relatives or colleagues. Call, write or email them as their champion. How would you like someone to champion you?

The wheel of life

You will almost certainly find that clients will regularly say that certain areas of their lives are fine, when they are actually hiding from, or keeping you from problems in that area. The use of the wheel of life can help your endeavour in being holistic and working with the client as a whole person.

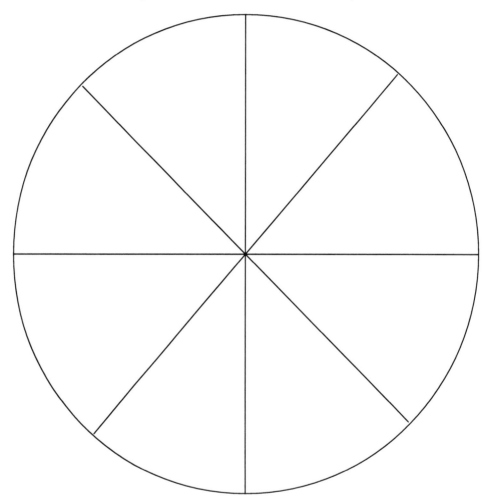

The process involves labelling each sector with an area of the person's life. For example, home, relationships, financial, career, spirituality, health, hobbies, friends. It can also be used to subdivide a particular area. For example career might be subdivided into different tasks, relationship with boss, relationship with subordinates, time management, progress opportunities etc.

Always ensure the subdivisions are appropriate for your client. For example if a person is not interested in spirituality then don't waste a sector!

The next step is to talk the client through the process of analysing how fulfilled they are in that particular area of their life. This can be done in hypnosis or not, depending on the client. Either you or the client then draws a line through the sector: the nearer the middle the less fulfilled, the nearer the edge, the more fulfilled. This then gives a picture of the client's life (or sublife). Awareness is the key, and you can use your intuition with this exercise to draw process from your client and to help create that awareness.

This then gives you information on which to work: which areas need attention? It is helpful to help your client to recognise that most sectors will be inter-related. For example, if they are fulfilled at home they are likely to be able to achieve more at work and if they are effective in work they are likely to be able to enjoy their free time more.

Exercise

Practice the wheel of life exercise for yourself and with friends.

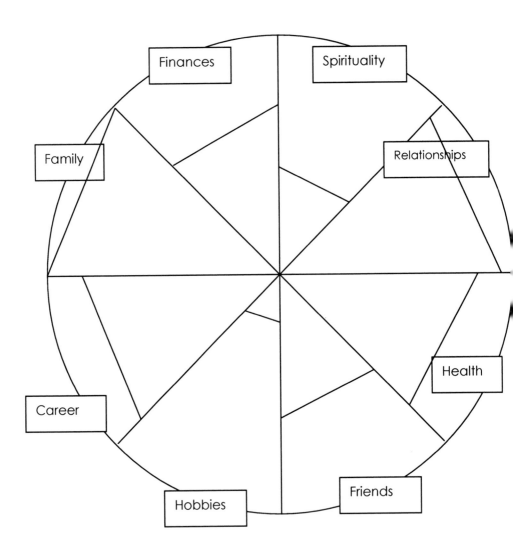

Finances

Spirituality

Family

Relationships

Career

Health

Hobbies

Friends

An example of the use of the wheel of life

Reframing

The basis of reframing is to separate intention from behaviour.

Two Major Types of Reframes:

CONTEXT REFRAME: "I'm too ...." -or- "He's too .... "

Think of a different context in which the person will respond differently to the same behaviour.

MEANING REFRAME: "Whenever 'X' happens, I respond 'Y'."

Ask yourself, "What else could this behaviour mean?" or internally think of an opposite frame or a different meaning. "What is it that this person hasn't noticed (in this context) that will bring about a different meaning, and change his response?"

Examples:

Reframe "I failed the exam because I am not good enough, and I never will be" to "I failed the exam because I believed I would, so didn't work hard enough. Next time I will do the work and I will pass".

Reframe "He said I was fat so I must lose a stone within two weeks" to "He said I was fat and I felt hurt. I don't know whether he was meaning to be insulting or helpful, but what matters is how I think. I will ask other's their opinion, and decide for myself whether I need to lose weight and tell him his comment hurt me."

Reframe "No man can be trusted" to "I have met some men who cannot be trusted, but I have also heard of some who can. I will be careful, but not presume."

Case example

Ted was suffering from work-related stress. He was a policeman and found that the depth of despair that he witnessed among some of the population was very difficult to cope with, Likewise he found that some of his colleagues had a cavalier attitude that he felt was disrespectful. Consequently he would be belittled at work, and then go home still feeling other people's pain and concerned at the attitudes displayed.

Ted's coach helped him, not only to deal with the emotional baggage of other people (through hypnosis and practical dissociation) but also to reframe his own "sensitivity" to a productive and beneficial sense of self. Ted learned that he was able to give the public an excellent service as he was able to empathise with their plights and also to recognize that just because colleagues displayed coldheartedness they did not necessarily feel that way. This may be their way of dealing with the same things that Ted had found difficult.

Modelling

A technique associated with NLP which is useful if not essential for hypnotic coaching is Modelling.

Modelling is how NLP came to be. In the 1970's Richard Bandler and John Grinder asked the question "Why were certain people successful in some fields, whilst others were not?". To discover why this was so, Bandler and Grinder decided to study certain giants. Milton Erickson, Virginia Satir and Fritz Perls were three of the people chosen to study. After some considerable research, Bandler and Grinder came up with a process called Modelling, which was a means of mechanistically "copying" what was important about these individuals and then installing their beliefs, values and behaviours in themselves, in order to make Bandler and Grinder more effective change agents.

The key elements in Modelling are matching and mirroring the physiology, filter patterns and strategies of the person one wants to model. The first element is modelling physiology, the key to which is breathing, and then modelling the posture. Great actors have been known to model these elements in order to make the portrayal of a character more realistic. The next is modelling the filter patterns. Filter patterns include things like values and beliefs. It is here we discover the emotional energy of the person being modelled. It is also here where many subjects for modelling are discovered to be inappropriate for us to model. Many years ago, Shaun had a mentor whom he went to great lengths to model. He spent a great deal of time with this individual, only to discover that this person's beliefs were so contrary to his own, that it was impossible for him to separate the values and beliefs from the reason he wanted to model this individual.

The final element is to elicit the strategy of how this person does what they do that makes the person a candidate for being modelled. In this aspect one may endeavour to find a model for one's business and another model for one's therapy, and so on. A model does not have to do everything well, just something that an individual would like to learn or become more effective at.

It is imperative to understand that modelling is not simple mimicry; it is the ability to separate what is essential from what is idiosyncratic. Additionally, you may have to take a significant behaviour and chunk it down into individual functions. For example, if one wanted to become the Chairman of ICI, one might first need to get the necessary education in order to do the job, which would be an individual function of a more significant behaviour.

Finally, a modeller needs feedback. It is essential that they get feedback regarding the modelling task. Also the modeller needs to know what the necessary mechanisms of the behaviour are and how they need to adjust them in order to maximise their success. To do this the modeller begins to start consciously dropping pieces of the strategy/behaviour to find out what is essential. Then using hypnosis one installs the behaviour/strategies into the modeller either through self or hetero means.

Case example

John was a 32 year old hypnotherapist who was seeing 1 or 2 clients per week. However he wanted to develop a profitable practice. He found a successful practitioner who he wanted to model and be coached by. He began by having a 3 hour interview with the model in question; at this stage John attempted to learn everything possible about how the model attracts clients. After this interview, the model gave John some tasks to complete in order to help him to build his practice based on the Model's business ethos.

One month later John reported an increase of his business of 100% meaning he was now seeing 4 clients per week. At this session, John elicited from his model what he finds to be critical about being a great hypnotherapist. The model replied, dedication to your craft, dedication to your clients, and dedication to yourself. John found these concepts slightly nebulous, but he asked if the model would do a hypnotic session in order to install these ideas in him.

After 18 months of bi-monthly meetings where John elicited more and more detail from his model. John was seeing 20 people per week and began a hypnotic DVD business. John was truly able to elicit the difference that made the difference for him.

Time management

Time is a matter of perception. This may seem odd at first, but just think of how time flies when you are having fun, or conversely drags when you aren't! Also it is well known that time is distorted in hypnosis. In Trevor Silvester's book "Wordweaving" he suggests that other occasions of time distortion show a trance like state where other hypnotic phenomena can be utilised. (eg post hypnotic suggestion).

So, it seems logical that for good time management we can utilise the ability to distort time for our benefit!

But of course, it isn't as simple as that, and specific steps can help.

One model is as follows:

SELECT
↓
EXCLUDE
↓
PERFORM

Selecting the task with the highest priority, excluding all others, and putting all one's effort into performing that task. The pattern is then repeated.

Here is a checklist for good time management:

- Make lists of EVERYTHING that you have to do, categorised into areas of your life.
- Plan each day thoroughly
- Mix your tasks to avoid boredom and promote energy
- Allow a good mix of work and breaks
- Build in flexibility to allow for the unexpected
- Always be on time
- Focus on one task at a time: only multitask when this doesn't reduce your effectiveness
- Delegate where possible
- Anticipate and adapt to change
- Give priority to important tasks. It can help to categorise the jobs on your list as high or low priority and whether they are big or small jobs. There may be a little gap in your schedule which could be filled with a

small, high priority job leaving big blocks of time for the bigger jobs
- Set clear, achievable goals
- Look after yourself
- Reward yourself
- Be honest with yourself
- Touch each piece of paper only once
- Avoid negativity
- Take time to exercise
- Don't procrastinate
- Finish one thing before moving on to another
- Learn to switch off
- Access emails once or twice a day and deal with each one as you read it (where possible)
- Learn to deal with interruptions, whether this is the phone (especially mobiles), visits or instant messaging. It is ok to be unavailable

Bad time management is essentially the inadequate use of time. One can take on too much, but that is another issue!

For example:

- A business man who drives into London when he could travel by train and work on the train
- An executive who schedules meetings with half hour gaps which aren't long enough to get into anything but too long just for a coffee
- An office worker who gets distracted by a chatty colleague
- A company owner who charges her time at £300 per day but does her own tax return
- A therapist who runs two clinics and is constantly running from one to the other rather than having blocks of time at each

Death bed scenario

This technique involves looking forward to your own death bed scene, and from there looking back.

NB: don't use this with people who are or could perceive themselves to be close to death, or who are depressed, or have little hope.

The aim is for them to see a fulfilled life, to feel happy with all they have done and achieved. This question gives them a chance to see what will make them complete.

Exercise

Ask some friends this question. How do they find it?

Assertiveness

Many clients will have problems being sufficiently assertive. This can be a complex issue, but can be started by a simple technique of helping your client to learn to say "no!".

Ask your client to list the last five times they said "yes", and then help them analyse exactly why they did so. Were these "appropriate" yeses? Or would it have been better for them to have said no? You may uncover potential guilt or a feeling that to say no would have been "letting someone down".

This may also lead to a greater awareness of the need to be liked and approved of. We all have this need of course, but it can be out of proportion to what is beneficial to the person.

Give the client the task of writing down every occasion in the next week where they say either yes or no to a request (obviously the more significant requests such as "will you come to the pub with me?", not "would you like fries with that?"!)

At the next session you can again analyse the responses, particularly any that are more unusual for the client, eg if they have dared to say no to something they usually say yes to!

Case example

Gaynor described herself as a doormat. She never said no, which meant that at work and home she was run ragged. She knew she was doing herself no favours, but she "feared confrontation". Her coach asked her about this in some detail and soon came to realise that Gaynor was actually expecting situations to become violent if she said no. This was puzzling to the coach as it was outside her experience, but she gently probed to find out why Gaynor had this perception. She was tempted to ask what circles Gaynor moved in that she expected her boss and best friend to hit her if she said she wouldn't take a memo to the next floor or go to an aerobics class, but she restrained.

Gaynor then revealed that she had witnessed what appeared to be an unprovoked attack on a young barman by the bar manageress when she had gone (illegally) to a pub at the age of 16. This had seriously upset her (there was a lot of blood, the lad was unconscious and an ambulance was called: she never discovered the outcome), and she had generalised this experience.

The coach was able to help Gaynor to get a more appropriate perspective, and while not discounting the possibility of random violence, to realise that it was exceedingly unlikely in the circumstances she was anticipating. Together they looked at more likely responses (anything from anger, to a sulk to nothing), and then Gaynor was able to try out new behaviours. The first two times, the others barely even noticed the no, and simply carried on!

Miracle question

This technique is designed to help a client see what needs to happen to move on or to solve a problem.

This is what you ask:

"Just imagine that after you have gone to bed tonight, a miracle happens and your problem is resolved. You are asleep while the miracle occurs. When you wake up tomorrow morning, what will tell you that the miracle has happened? What will be different? How? What will you be doing differently? What will others be doing differently?"

This gives the client clues as to the steps they need to take.

Case example

Juliette was having problems with her teenage daughter, Tasha. There was little communication and what there was tended to be antagonistic, in both directions. The coach used the Miracle Question. Here is Juliette's response:

"I go downstairs and Tasha is in the kitchen. She says "Morning, Mum" and smiles. I say "Morning, Darling" and give her a kiss on the cheek. We have breakfast together and I ask her what her plans for the day are. Tasha tells me she is going to town with her best friend, and asks if I could meet her later to help her choose a dress for a party. I feel relaxed and happy. I feel connected to Tasha."

This response enables the coach and Juliette together to look at what it is that is preventing this connection between the two of them. To cut a long story short, Juliette is then able to talk to Tasha about what is going on, and it transpires that each was feeling unloved by the other.

I-CAN-DO

This model of coaching has been taken from "The Life Coaching Handbook" by Curly Martin.

The acronym stands for:

Investigate
Current
Aims
Number
Date
Outcome

And is a model to follow through any coaching session. Here is an example of its use:

I: What is your reason for wanting to run a marathon?
C: How far can you run comfortably now?
A: What is your aim, completion or is the time important?
N: How many ways can you think to get more training in?
D: When do you want to do this?
O: How will it feel when you achieve this?

Letting go

Clients will often find themselves stuck. Either stuck in an old pattern, stuck with an old emotion, or just unable to move on following a change that has been forced upon them.

Here the Sedona method is very useful. This is a complex method of reducing stress, and we will present just a snapshot here of the process of letting go. See resources section for where to find more information.

The basic model has three simple steps:

1. Relax and allow yourself to feel whatever it is you feel. Really allow it, welcome it if possible, but really let the feeling be there
2. Ask yourself the following questions:
    a. Could you let it go?
    b. Would you?
    c. When?

This system can work with any feelings, including positive ones (it makes them stronger).

Breaking Chains

Chains are what tie us down, hold us back, keep us connected to past habits. They can be seen as self-limiting beliefs.

Here are some examples of chains:

- I have to support my mother
- I don't deserve a good job
- I fear failure
- I can't stop thinking about whether my ex might take me back so I keep emailing and popping round, just in case

Here are some ways to break chains:

1. Ask yourself what a loved one would say about your chain. Eg. would your mother agree that you should hold yourself back to support her? What would other family members say about it?
2. Use affirmations to counteract the chain. Eg. Say out loud 10 times each morning and 10 times at night "I deserve a good job"
3. Talk to yourself in the mirror. Eg. Discuss with your reflection the chance of failing and the implications if you did. Look at best and worse case scenarios.
4. Use the Viking principle: ie burn your boats. Eg. Decide to cut off all connection. No more emails or calls. If he wants you he knows where you are.

Panning for Gold

This technique is one that can be useful for anyone, but particularly for clients who are negative or going through a bad patch. The idea is, each night before sleep, to review the day, "panning for gold".

Just as if you were really panning for gold, there will be nuggets of gold amongst the mud. These are the good things, maybe just a smile, a kind word, a pleasant memory or the sight of a flower, but they will be there. There may be lots of "mud", but this can simply wash through the sieve leaving the nuggets of gold there to be appreciated.

Here is an example of the nuggets (a list produced by a regular coaching client of one of the authors at the time of writing this chapter):

- The feel of the warm water in the shower
- The taste of that first cup of coffee in the morning
- A kiss on the cheek from my son as he left for school
- A surprise visit at work from a colleague who recently had a baby. I held a tiny hand.
- A two-for-one bargain on my favourite shampoo
- Treating myself to a peach smoothie
- The word "thanks" from a difficult client
- The bus arriving on time and not being full
- Peace and quiet while cooking the dinner
- Watching a new comedy
- Reading Fox in Socks to the children and getting the giggles

Being popular

Many clients will have issues to do with relationships, whether with partners, family, colleagues, friends or even strangers. In fact couldn't everyone find some area here that could be better? It is therefore useful if you can give guidance on how to relate, and to be popular. Here are some of the key ideas:

- Listen! We have two ears and one mouth, so use them in proportion. Everyone likes to be listened to, everyone likes to feel that they are interesting, so be curious and they will appreciate it
- Consider what you say from the other person's perspective. Do you say things that may offend? Or do you have mannerisms that may offend? For example, swearing is still offensive to some people, and stating hard line views on politics or religion is bound to offend at times
- Make good eye contact, but don't stare!
- There is no need to entertain. Just be you.
- Use compliments, but make them real, and use them sparingly. One of the authors has a friend who always says "haven't you lost weight?" when he sees her. She now realises that this either means that he just says it because he thinks people like it, or that he perceives her as heavier than she is. Neither of which is endearing.
- Remember your previous meetings and conversations. This shows that you value the other person. It shows respect and people like people who respect them.
- Do not presume that other people will remember these things though. You will appear modest (which is an attractive trait), if you ask someone if they remember rather than jumping to the conclusion that they must (even if you would feel insulted if they had indeed forgotten)

- Be generous with yourself and your time. If its possible then be generous with your money too, but this is less important. Having said that, the quickest route to being unpopular is "not to pay for your round".
- Also be generous with positivity and encouragement. There is always something you can say that will be a gift to the other person
- Avoid being rude (and by this we don't mean just critical, but out and out mean!) about other people. The person you are talking to may worry that you talk about <u>them</u> like that when you are with others (and you probably do, if this is something you do at all!)

Transactional analysis

TA is absolutely chock-a-block with jargon: so please forgive us for using it! If you are interested in the concepts, you may be interested to read more.

Scripts, Injunctions & Patterns

A script is the way a person lives their life. It is set up in childhood as a strategy to ensure the best chance of survival, based on the child's perception. The child decides how best to live and can make their script very complex. But we will look at two of the basic elements of life scripting.

Firstly, everyone lives the majority of the time from one of four positions:

1. I'm ok, you're ok
2. I'm ok, you're not ok
3. I'm not ok, you're ok
4. I'm not ok, you're not ok

Secondly there are some standard scripts that many people have as part of theirs:

- Be perfect
- Be strong
- Try hard
- Please people
- Hurry up

Injunctions are the opposite of scripts. Here are some typical ones:

- Don't make it
- Don't grow up
- Don't think
- Don't be well
- Don't be
- Don't do anything
- Don't be close
- Don't be you
- Don't be important
- Don't feel
- Don't be a child
- Don't belong

Patterns are scripty phrases that many people live by. For example

- I can't have fun <u>until</u> I've finished my work
- I can have fun today but I'll pay for it <u>later</u>
- I can <u>never</u> get what I want most
- Why does this <u>always</u> happen to me?
- I <u>almost</u> made it this time
- I made it this time but it wasn't <u>good enough</u>

Or how about a combination:

- I can't have fun <u>until</u> I've finished, but I <u>never</u> finish so I get no fun!

The Drama Triangle

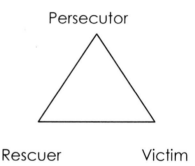

All these positions are maladaptive and inauthentic: their capital letters indicate that they are roles and not reality (although the person occupying the role may perceive it as real, a sort of bogus reality).

Persecutors believe themselves to be ok and others not. They need Victims to Persecute.
Rescuers also believe themselves to be ok and others not. They need Victims to Rescue.
Victims believe themselves to be not ok and others to be ok. They need Persecutors to persecute them and are looking for Rescuers to rescue them.

Exercise

Can you think of cases where someone could be described by these titles but not with a Capital letter?

Games

Games are maladaptive means of getting one's needs met. The concept was introduced in the book "Games People Play" by Eric Berne, written in 1964.

Games are repetitive interactions following rules but played without awareness. They always end up with players feeling a familiar emotion that is based in childhood and are inappropriate for adulthood.

Let's give some examples of games to explain the process:

Why Don't You, Yes But.

In this game one player sets up the other to offer advice and then rejects each option. To end the game there is usually a switch into blaming the advisor as being useless or to reinforce the victim mentality.

If you get a client like this (or rather when...) you can cut across their pattern using the triple negative technique. This technique sounds ridiculous and needs practice. Let's say you want to suggest that the client asks her husband to help with the washing up (when you would expect a "yes but he might get cross" or similar response). Using the triple negative you say "No. You wouldn't want to ask him to help you wouldn't you?". She will do it!

135

Wooden leg

This is another game played by Victims. They constantly "say" in one way or another "I can't do that because I have got a wooden leg/wasn't loved by my mother/am female or some other reason. They will continue avoiding in this way and receiving strokes for their "poor me" attitude until challenged. They then switch into persecutor of the challenger.

Gee, you are wonderful professor

This game is one that all therapists should be wary of! The player will set someone up, typically an advisor/professional of some sort as being THE one who can help. Perhaps they've tried everyone else, or they have heard wonderful things. But this is just a game. The professional is set up to fail so that the instigator can then belittle them. This gives them a feeling of superiority and importance.

Exercise

Who do you know who plays games? Do you?

The Ego-state Model

This model states that at any time each person is either in Parent, Adult or Child mode.

- Parent is acting as one's parents did and can be termed "controlling" or "nurturing".

- Adult is using current information and resources to choose appropriate behaviour.

- Child is behaving as one did as a child and can be termed "adapted" or "free".

All these ego-states have their place, and can be appropriate.

For example:
- Being in controlling parent mode may be appropriate for a police officer dealing with a drunken lout.
- Being in nurturing parent mode may be appropriate for a nurse with a frightened patient.
- Being in free child mode might be appropriate for a honeymooning couple running on a beach.
- Being in adapted child mode might be appropriate for someone having tea with the Queen (remembering their manners!)

BUT they can be inappropriate:

For example:
- Being in controlling parent mode when dealing with a late employee.
- Being in nurturing parent mode by doing someone else's work for them when all they needed was a hand.

- Being in free child mode when driving a motorbike down a crowded road.
- Being in adapted child mode when discussing an ailment with your GP.

As a coach you will hear your client give you examples of these. Examples may be of their own inappropriate behaviour, which can then be challenged using the model, or typically in how they are relating to others. Perhaps a boss who is treating them as from Parent to Child, or a real parent who will not communicate Adult to Adult.

TA therapists use the term crossed transactions for when communication is not parallel. This, when used in awareness, can be a very useful tool.

To use the examples above, if the boss speaks to your client as parent to Child, the client can deliberately respond as Adult to Adult. The result is one of two things: either the boss is forced to shift to a parallel communication, or the communication breaks down. The same would apply with the other example.

A complication to this theory is that of "Ulterior transactions". An example is of a salesperson who explains that a product is top of the range, but probably out of the customer's price range. This, on a surface level, seems to be an adult to adult communication, but at a deeper level the salesperson is communicating to the customer's Child, hoping to push them into a child like response of "I'll take it!"

Further Reading Recommendations:

TA Today: Ian Stewart and Vann Joines
This is a standard text that overviews the TA concepts. Very readable and usable as a "manual"

I'm OK You're OK: Thomas Harris
A book that can be used by anyone to gain an understanding of TA concepts. A very full but readable book. Can be found in the "Pop Psychology" sections of bookshops, even now after 35 years!

Games People Play: Eric Berne
The original book on which all TA is based. It is divided into two sections, the first giving some of the primary concepts, then a "dictionary" of the games that Berne "discovered". A little dated, but a must if you like these ideas.

Existentialism

Existential Givens

There are four existential givens, and struggling with any or all produces what is known as existential angst:

- Death is inevitable
- Everyone is ultimately alone
- We are free to make of our lives as we will
- There is no obvious meaning or sense to life

Human Rights

There are some fundamental human rights, but you'll be amazed how many people don't recognise them, for themselves and/or for others. In fact often they will see others as having these rights and forget they have them too.

In a moment we will list some basic human rights, but first it is worth saying that with rights come responsibilities, and tights can never be considered to be complete and absolute. For example, we state that people have a right to have needs met, but who then has the duty to meet them? The right to express feelings may conflict with another person's rights. As you can see this area is full of philosophical and practical issues, but let's use this as a starting point:

All people have the right:

- To be
- To be separate
- To be autonomous
- To grow
- To change

140

- To need AND to be independent
- To have needs met
- To assert themselves
- To love and be loved
- To be free and lovingly committed
- To be treated with respect
- To be respected as an equal human being
- To say yes or no for ourselves
- To express our feelings and opinions
- To make mistakes
- To change our minds
- To say "I don't know"
- To decline responsibility for the actions of others

Exercise

Do you agree? How do you fare on these things?

Monitoring and Reviewing

Accountability

Aha! This is a biggy. All the coaching books talk about how the client needs to be accountable, and most give tips on how to achieve this. Often these tips include making the client feel beholden to you so that they agree to what you suggest and do what they have agreed. Also they talk about ensuring that the client is motivated to achieve and that they set appropriate goals.

These ideas are all absolutely fine, of course, but ultimately the clients ARE accountable only to themselves, as we all are in life. Part of what you will be encouraging will be autonomy for your clients; you must beware of promoting this with one hand and taking it back with the other.

So, this is a difficult line to walk, and we suggest that you bring this factor into the open as soon as possible and often if necessary!

Self-sabotage

We could write a book on this topic (Hey! That's an idea!), but we will keep it simple here. The important thing is that you recognise that EVERYONE sabotages themselves in some ways at some times. It is only the degree and method that varies.

Exercise

Make a random list of people you know, knew or are famous. See if you can think of a time you know of when they have sabotaged themselves. What would you say to them if you were their coach at the time?

Case example

Hugh had landed his "perfect job"; one he had been going after for several years. It was the ultimate! But he immediately started to sabotage it by being late, working inefficiently and being unwilling to listen to advice that he was given by not only his coach but the boss and his colleagues who were all trying to help him.

In his coaching sessions Hugh was very negative. The job was "not all it was cracked up to be", he had been "misled" and it was all "unfair". His coach felt unsettled by this sudden negativity and "moany" attitude, and yet Hugh seemed almost happy to whine, and reported doing so at home and in the office too.

This was very tricky for the coach, as Hugh closed down to him and was unreceptive to any approach. It took many sessions before progress was made, and by this time Hugh was close to losing the job, and his wife. He was suffering from stress-related illnesses and life looked bleak.

The turning point came when the coach noticed the use of a particular phrase that was repeated several times in the session. This was "they all think I am weak". It was one of those situations when the coach used intuition and the timing worked. He asked "who thinks you are weak?". Hugh burst into tears and reported that it was his grandfather (long since deceased), who had scorned his attempts to do anything as a child.

This was a revelation to Hugh because although he knew that his grandfather had been this way, he was not aware of the impact. Time line regression was used to re-evaluate his experiences, Gestalt techniques (in trance) employed to deal with the relationship, and then Hugh and is coach were able to "go back to square one" to help him look at his future.

Influencing factors

We will now cover some areas that are likely to become apparent as factors at this stage: ie after goals are set and interventions applied. Of course, they may be immediately apparent to either you, the coach or the client.

Parenting

Many of your clients will be parents and whether or not they have "problems" with their children, their role as a parent is likely to be a part of their life that is brought into discussions. It may be a primary focus or a secondary one.

The more you understand about child development the better, but this cannot form part of this book!

Further Reading Recommendations:

John Bowlby and Attachment Theory: Jeremy Holmes
A text book about the theories espoused by John Bowlby. Readable and very useful for gaining understanding of those who struggle with all sorts of relationships as adults.

The Continuum Concept: Jean Liedloff
A lovely book discussing how other cultures bring up their children and how we can incorporate their ideas into our society.

Childhood and Society: Erik H Erikson
A classic, but rather "heavy" text. Maybe one to borrow from the library before buying to see if it suits you!

Playing and Reality: Donald Winnicott
A book on object relations theory which introduces the concept of the good enough mother. Worth reading for this

alone. The concept is amazingly useful with clients who are either struggling to separate from their parents or who are parents themselves.

The Interpersonal World of the Infant: Daniel Stern
This book looks at the development of the concept of self. This is a process which often is flawed and results in faulty self-concepts. Again a knowledge of the processes can help you to understand your clients.

The Drama of Being a Child: Alice Miller
Another classic, but easy to read.

Dibbs: In Search of Self: Virginia Axline
A case history of the use of play therapy with one boy. Inspiring!

The TA books mentioned previously are also good sources of information on child development.

However much, or little, you know about child development and generally about bringing up children, it is just as important in this area as in any other that you do not impose your views on your client.

You may believe that it is immoral to smack a child, but if your client disagrees they have a right to make their choice. As with all issues of right and wrong there will be disagreements about where to draw the line. You need to be clear that the mark has been overstepped and so, if they give you good reason to believe that they are abusing a child then you are duty bound, and bound by law to act.

Let's get back to the more likely scenario that a client gives you reason to believe that if they modified the way they were behaving with the child, then it would be beneficial all round. You need to be careful of your phrasing, and extended quotes can be helpful here. This is an example:

"Just last week I was at a seminar where the presenter talked about a client of his, who read a book which said that children liked to be treated in an adult-like way and given the responsibility to make simple choices, such as whether to wear a coat or not or what to have for breakfast".

Using this sort of phrasing (and it doesn't need to be true!) means that your client will have no idea who is saying that children like autonomy; they will just hear the idea and are much more likely to accept it. There are however, some people who will hear whatever you say as being your view whether it is or not so beware of this possibility!

To finish this brief segment, let us share with you an insight that has proved very valuable to the authors' work with many clients. Parents often have a "Be Perfect" script when it comes to parenting. But, paradoxically, a perfect parent would be imperfect: perfection would not teach the child about the real world. Therefore, being imperfect and making mistakes is actually good for the child! An awareness of this fact can really take the pressure off.

Case example

Jenny is a single parent with twins of six. She is an Estate Agent and works long hours. She employs a nanny to look after the girls. She has sought coaching to help her with her work/life balance. The twins have been "playing up". At school they relate only to each other, and are reluctant to follow the teacher's instructions.

The coach has explained that she is not an expert in child behaviour, and she and Jenny agree to work on Jenny's behaviour to see how this affects the children. At the time of writing some progress has been made. Jenny has employed an extra assistant at the office and it is now a self-imposed rule that she takes the children to school herself, and then goes to the office. The nanny still collects the girls, but Jenny is always home in time to have a meal with them at 6 which the nanny has prepared.

The cost of the extra agent has been mostly covered by the savings on the cost of the nanny, and Jenny is feeling that she is happier to be spending more time with the girls. She also feels that because of her strict time boundaries, she is more focussed at the office and better able to delegate.

Her gut feeling is that the children are happier and is looking forward to discussing their progress at school at parents' evening at the end of term in four weeks.

Problem parents

All parents are problems! That may seem a sweeping statement, but the process of separation from one's parents, and the process of recognising that they are not perfect is often a difficult one to negotiate. A good book on this subject is "In and out of the garbage pail" by Fritz Perls. The essence is that in order to get to a point of living an autonomous life, separate from one's parents one has to accept them for what they are and how they were with you, warts and all. This is the process of throwing them in the garbage pail. Only once they are in there can you bring them out again and establish a full strength adult to adult relationship with them.

Many clients will be bringing parental issues, often under the surface. Here is a questionnaire that you can use with them to help ascertain where they are in the process. Awareness, as usual, is the key to allowing for change.

In my relationship with my parents, I believe that:

- My parents could not survive without me
- I could not survive without my parents
- It is my job to keep my parents contented
- I am responsible for my parents
- If I do not make my parents proud, I have failed
- My parents expect certain things from me and if I don't provide them they would be devastated
- My parents are stronger than me
- I should not upset my parents
- I cannot tell my parents everything about me for fear of their reaction
- They would not listen to me
- If they knew how much they had hurt me I would feel better

- My parents always did their best and that is all that matters
- I fight with my parents all the time

If the client ticks more than three of these, there is work to do!

Here again we find ourselves looking at appropriate responsibility. Here are some things your client was not responsible for:

- Being neglected/ignored/abused/bullied
- Being treated as unloved or unlovable
- Other people's cruelty
- Other people's problems
- Other people's unhappiness
- Other people's choices

But your client is responsible for how he felt then and feels now. The past is unchangeable and those reactions are as they were. But there is choice from this point on.

Case example

Duane was 25 when he had coaching at work. His boss was unhappy with his lack of willingness to accept authority, but Duane said that he wasn't going to take instructions from idiots (not his actual word!). It transpired that he had had problems throughout his childhood with an abusive, alcoholic father.

It was clear to both coach and client that some work on his past was needed in order to enable Duane to move forward.

The coach explained the theory of transference and this was helpful as a temporary measure to help Duane to recognise that his boss was not his father and should therefore not be treated as such.

Much work was done about Duane's past and current relationships with both parents, giving Duane the opportunity to establish a situation that was as "good as it was ever going to be", according to Duane. This also enabled him to develop good relationships outside the family, not just at work but socially too.

This is an excellent example of how hypnotic coaching is more effective than either hypnotherapy or coaching alone as it is a holistic approach to the client's whole life.

Sex-roles and gender differences

Surprisingly enough your clients will be either male or female and will have been brought up in a culture where certain things are expected from each gender. Some may try to pretend otherwise, but this is unavoidable. Everybody will also receive conflicting messages.

As an exercise, one of the authors called her children, two boys then aged 8 and 10, into the office at this point in writing and asked them what was different about how boys and girls are and in what they do. She would like to point out that she and her husband make a concerted effort to encourage a perception of equality between the sexes!

Here are their responses:

Boys	Girls
Strong	Care about not breaking nails
Older boys don't cry	Cry more
Can do as well in exams if they try	Do better in exams
Shouldn't wear dresses	Can wear trousers
If both sexes in a car the man would drive	Drive more sensibly
Get into trouble more	Goody two shoes
Better at football, rugby	Good at hockey, netball, athletics
Good at fast dancing	Good at slow dancing
Aren't secretaries/cleaners	Aren't builders/fire fighters
Cook professionally	Cook as a hobby

The crucial aspect of this is to recognise that your client will have perceptions about their role as a man/woman, and of the role of others, including you. It can help to ascertain what these expectations are and, if necessary to challenge them.

152

Interestingly, in the above example, the boys got into discussions between themselves (without their mother's intervention as she was trying to keep focussed!), about the validity of their observations, often deciding that they were not actually true, or need not be.

Exercise

Open yourself to an awareness of any prejudices you may have. Can you admit to them, even if just to yourself?

Case example

Flora was working in IT and doing well. She had received several promotions but always had an underlying feeling that her gender was interfering with her progress. She felt resentful.

Her coach wanted to know more as she had an intuitive feeling that perhaps there was more to this than met the eye. It can be easy to presume that the client's perception of "reality" is "true". In this case it turned out that Flora had won promotion in two recent cases when the other candidates were all male and the interviewers were likewise all male.

When asked for an example of this "unfair treatment", Flora told the story of when she had fought her corner in a meeting, and the boss had replied with "how can anyone with earrings like those be taken seriously?" *

However, her view was accepted. It seemed to the coach that perhaps the boss's statement was actually said with affection, but Flora had missed this. The relationship was such that she felt able to raise this possibility and it was one that Flora had not considered. Following some in depth work it turned out that what Flora had been perceiving as "sexism" was only partly so. She is a tiny person who looks very delicate and so many people (women as well as men) would find their natural reaction was to "look after" her, which of course in business was not what she wanted, nor appropriate.

However, it had NOT interfered with her progress in any way which was discernable. It seems that Flora had already developed her own way of getting over this and ensuring that she was treated as an effective member of the team. All she needed was to recognise that this is how things were.

*for those who care about such things, the earrings were baskets of fruit..... but this was in the early 90's

Other role issues

Your client will come to you with a whole set of roles that he or she will adopt from time to time. It can be of great importance to explore these roles and ascertain where conflicts arise and where improvements can be made.

Roles include:

Job titles   Family positions   Friendships
Societal positions Hobbies

As an example, Fiona can list the following as just some of her roles:

Coach, Counsellor, Hypnotherapist, Supervisor, Supervisee, Colleague, Chair, Director, Student, Wife, Mother, Friend, Daughter, Sister, Neighbour, Writer, Customer, Painter, Spectator.

Special consideration can apply to roles in which the associated tasks are unclear, or where the roles and/or tasks change.

For example, if a client takes on a new job that has an unclear job description, or becomes a mother for the first time, there can be difficulties to adapting to the role. Or a client may be in the process of divorce that changes their role from wife to ex-wife, and the associated tasks also change. If another's perception of their role does not also change, confusion follows.

Case example

Geoff was going through a divorce. It was an amicable divorce and one agreed on both sides. Geoff had moved out of the family home, but kept being "pulled back" to do jobs such as mowing the lawn and fixing things. When there his wife treated him exactly as she had when he was still living there (ie as a husband), to the extent that they would often have sex too.

This lead Geoff to feel very confused. Was he a husband or an ex-husband? His coach helped him to analyse his roles, what they meant and how he wanted them to be so that he was able to fully take on his new role. It was not an easy process as his wife took some convincing that this was necessary, but they have both now moved on with their lives and both feel positive about the outcome.

Emotions

Worry

Worry can be good. It can help a client to prepare for an event, to do their best, to avoid problems. But it can get out of hand, causing confusion and an inability to order thoughts. It can build and become overwhelming. In fact the reasonable, beneficial level of worry is better called concern.

You can worry about
    yourself
    others
    things

In the
    past
    present
    future

Some of these can be looked at differently. For example there is no point worrying about the past at all, but you can think through past events, learn from them and take action based on this learning.

Worrying about your child's safety is logical but only up to a point. If your child is 40 and you are worried about his holiday in Spain, this may be overdoing it!

Worrying about your car can again be logical in that it may ensure that you keep it well maintained. If you still worry then this indicates a problem (with you rather than with the car!).

Here are some ideas to use with worry:

BE CLEAR

1. Get the client to write down *exactly* what they are worried about and how the items are a problem.
2. Tackle the items on the list one by one. Question their accuracy and truth.
3. Look for one thing they can do about each item on the list.
4. Select one of these that they can succeed at easily.
5. Decide a time at which they can take that action.
6. Get them to report back after having taken the action.

Another idea is to task the client to write down a list of their worries at the end of each day, and on the same day the next week, review the list. The chances are that they will soon learn that they are worrying about things unnecessarily

WORST CASE SCENARIO

1. Ask the client what is the worst that can happen (realistically!).
2. Get them to imagine the worst happening, or role-play it with them if appropriate.
3. See how it is for them, and ask how they imagine coping.
4. Get them to write down their feelings and responses.
5. Now look at what is *likely* to happen.
6. Ask them how they will cope with that.
7. Look at how much responsibility they have about what will happen.
8. If it is up to them, use "Be Clear" above, if not, then use other techniques, as appropriate

Fear

Fear is a normal emotion and one that is necessary for life. To have no fear is incredibly dangerous. But again it needs to be balanced.

The unconscious mind cannot differentiate between real and imagined fear, hence someone's reaction to an armed robber can be the same as their reaction to a TV image of a snake. The adrenaline reaction produces the same symptoms.

There are some forms of fear that you may need to deal with (in the clients or in you?)

Fear of failure

The fear of failure is one of the greatest blocks to achievement. To many people the phrase "It is better to have loved and lost than never to have loved at all" makes no sense. For them it can be infinitely preferably not to take the risk of hurt.

For these clients, getting them to take action can be difficult and the "Worst Case" exercise above can help.

An example of this was a client who was fearful of rejection and so would not put herself forward for promotion. Her coach helped her to realise how this was holding her back and causing frustration, and so the next time a better job became available, she made the choice to put everything into getting it. She didn't, and the rejection hurt a lot. But (and it's a big but), she knew she had survived, and she was proud to have gone for it in such a way. A few months later an even better job was advertised and she went for it again, and got it.

Fear of success

Conversely you will find that some clients have a fear of success. This may seem odd, but there can be many reasons and it is important not to second guess what the client's reason may be. But it could be due to

- A belief that they don't deserve it
- A fear of how they will be perceived
- A fear of having then to repeat the success
- A fear of failure following the success (eg it's safer to fail as there isn't then a drop)

Irrational

Irrational fears may include phobias and disproportionate ideas. For example a client may be afraid of flying. The first question to ask is whether they are afraid of flying or crashing. The first is a phobia, the second is disproportionate. As a hypnotic coach you are equipped to deal with both types of fear.

How to overcome fear

Go through the following procedure. Get the client to use paper (write down the answers yourself too), and be specific. Example answers are given alongside

1. What outcome do you want?

Answer: I want to be able to make a speech at my sister's wedding

2. Why? What pain will this avoid or what gain will you get?

Answer: I will avoid the pain of embarrassment at not doing and get the gain of feeling proud.

3. What rules do you need to set?

Answer: Firstly that I can make my choice, secondly that I can use keywords on cards, and thirdly that I can have no more that two drinks first!

4. What is the best possible outcome?

Answer: People laugh and my sister is pleased

5. What is the worst possible outcome?

Answer: People laugh at me!

6. What is the likely outcome?

Answer: Most people don't pay much attention and my sister is pleased

7. Write out your decision in the form of "I've decided to..."

Answer: I have decided to make the speech

8. Say this out loud.

9. Write down: "I am allowed to feel the nerves and to enjoy them!"

10. Say this out loud.

Exercise

Try the above exercise with an example of your own; real if possible, but if not, imagine a scenario in which you would be afraid.

Guilt and Shame

Guilt and shame are fascinating emotions! Some say they are merely means of control by society: a way of preventing members of society from disobeying its rules.

Who has not had that feeling of "I'd better not…..because if I did I would feel awful"?

In this role, guilt and shame can be very effective. But they are "stick" rather than "carrot" motivators. It is important to differentiate between appropriate and inappropriate feelings of guilt and shame, and those feeling which are generated internally or those imposed by others.

In the coaching relationship, these emotions often provide blocks to progression, sometimes through an inability to get over old guilt, sometimes through fear of encountering the emotions again.

An example of the first might be a client who once caused a colleague to lose their job, simply by being much more efficient and creating an awareness of the inadequacies of the other person. They hold on to an inappropriate feeling of guilt and stay trapped.

An example of the second might be a client who had an affair and felt so guilty for the pain he caused his wife that he is unwilling to risk feeling this again and so will not approach his wife to discuss problems in the marriage.

The coach's role with these emotions is one of exploration, understanding, and encouragement to allow clients to forgive themselves and to move on without fear.

Grief

Grief is really a mixture of emotions, but a mixture that a coach may well have to assist a client to deal with. It may not be their primary presenting issue or a perceived relevant factor at the outset but it may be underlying or, of course, arise during the course of your work with a client. One of the authors of this course recently had the experience of a client whose mother died the day after the client admitted for the first time that she was angry with her. A coach needs to be prepared to deal with whatever happens in the client's life, and have a system of referral in place when they are out of their depth.

REMEMBER! Grief can be felt over any loss: of a person whether or not they have died, an animal, a thing, a relationship or a part of the self (youth/body part/role).

There are four tasks of mourning:

1. To accept the reality of the loss
2. To experience the pain of grief
3. To adjust to the changed environment
4. To withdraw emotional energy & to re-invest it elsewhere

Here are some of the symptoms of grief. The crucial thing is for the client to be aware that these symptoms are normal.

Feelings	Thoughts	Behaviour	Physical Symptoms
Anxiety	Disbelief	Searching	Appetite change
Sadness	Preoccupation	Over-activity	Awareness of noise
Tiredness	Confusion	Sleep disturbance	Breathlessness
Shock	Sense of presence	Avoidance	Emptiness
Guilt	Hallucinations	Absent mindedness	Dry mouth
Anger		Sighing	Listlessness
Pining		Treasuring of things	Sore throat
Relief		Crying	Weakness
Self-reproach		Withdrawal	
Loneliness		Dreaming	
Helplessness			
Emancipation			

Stress

Remember: stress is not necessarily bad; in fact we need it and it can be positive as well as negative. Good stress is sometimes called eustress.

Everyone reacts to stress differently. Having said that, it is traditional to use a chart such as the one below to analyse the stresses in an individual's life. We would advise caution and that you always check out the appropriateness of a score. For example the gain of a new family member may for some be exceedingly stressful but for others no more than a stroll in the park.

Score	Life Event	Score	Life Event
100	Death of a spouse	29	Change in responsibilities at work
73	Divorce	29	Son or daughter leaving home
65	Marital separation	29	Trouble with in laws
63	Jail term	28	Outstanding personal achievement
63	Death of a close family member	26	Partner stops or starts work
53	Personal injury or illness	25	Change in living conditions
50	Marriage	24	Revision of personal habits
47	Fired at work	23	Trouble with boss

45	Retirement	20	Change in work conditions
44	Change in health of family member	20	Change in residence
40	Pregnancy	19	Change in recreation
39	Sex difficulties	19	Change in church activities
39	Gain of a new family member	18	Change in social activities
39	Business readjustment	17	Loan for lesser purchase
38	Change in financial state	16	Change in sleeping habits
37	Death of a close friend	15	Change in family get-togethers
36	Change to different line of work	15	Change in eating habits
35	More arguments with spouse	13	Vacation
31	Mortgage or major loan	12	Christmas
30	Foreclosure of mortgage or loan	11	Minor violations of the law

To calculate a score, take the number of times an event occurred and multiply by its score, then total all scores.

150-199   37% chance of stressors leading to illness or
disease within a year
200-299   51%   "

300+   79%   "

Exercise

Try this exercise for yourself, right now! What do you think
of the presumptions within? How do you feel this could be
used with clients?

Monitoring progress

Measuring

In the same way that we have referred to the fact that if you do not know where you are going you are unlikely to get there, so it is crucial to measure the effectiveness of the steps you are taking to get there.

An analogy would be making a journey and telling your friend at the other end that you will be there by dinner time. You then plan the trip, getting at least a rough idea of when you need to leave, the route you will take and how long you can stop for on the way.

It is then obvious that you pay attention en route to your progress. You will watch for road signs, change your route if you go wrong, and probably decide not to divert to visit somewhere else on the way for a few hours.

In the same way, your clients need to keep track of where they are on their path, and whether they are keeping to time.

The initial planning is critical to this process. If, for example, a client says I will be a millionaire, but doesn't say when or how, measuring progress is tricky. But if they have mapped out that by contacting x businesses each week, converting y into a contract, each worth £z, then progress can be accurately measured and changes made to the plan if required.

Some goals however, may be less specific. For example a person who is unhappy in their marriage may want things to improve. In these cases scales can be used. This is a very simple but effective way of measuring progress. In this example the client may say that they are at 2 on a scale of 0 to 10 where 0 represents the unhappiest, and 10 absolute bliss. If they then make a note of their score every day, and there is a general upward trend then progress is being measured.

Gap Analysis

Gap analysis describes the difference between current results and consequences (the reality) and desired results and consequences (the vision), the difference between the "as is" and the "to be."

Cause analysis is the process of determining the root cause of past, present, and future performance gaps. What are some of the causes of gaps?
- Lacking in behaviours: skills and knowledge, individual capacity, motivation and expectations.
- Lacking in environmental support: environment support, resources and tools, data, information and feedback, consequences, incentives and rewards.

Checking validity of goals

It is not uncommon for clients to aim for goals that could be described as invalid. What does invalid mean?

- A goal that is designed to meet an inappropriate need (eg a 50 year old wanting a dead father's approval)
- A goal that is designed to meet an appropriate need, inappropriately (eg losing weight by eating grapefruit only)
- A goal that is designed to avoid meeting the real need (eg aiming to earn a million when the real need is to be loved)
- A goal that is designed to create success for the sake of it (eg enrolling on a course that is too easy and gives no benefit)

These are a few examples; bear in mind that this is always something to look out for when working with your clients.

So, it is important that the purpose of the goal, the need it is aiming to meet and the reasons behind it are monitored.

This is one of the most fundamental roles of a coach. You are in a position (if you dare!) to question the client's reasons and to help them to become aware of their blind spots. In a recent presentation in a coaching class, two of the students role-played a client of 42 who wanted to be in Popstars the Rivals of the Rivals. This was an invalid goal, and the coach's job was to point this out, gently but effectively.

Often of course, the validity or otherwise of a goal is not so obvious, so gentle probing and monitoring is the best course of action.

Exercise

Being as honest with yourself as you can be, use this to
evaluate your own goals.

Looking at obstacles

We have looked at various sorts of barriers before, in the
sections on breaking chains and self-sabotage for example,
but here we are going to look specifically at barriers to
achieving goals.

Let's look at the following formula:

Success = goal + movement + resources – obstacles

If we use a football analogy, success (scoring), requires a
goal (literally), movement of the player, resources (ie a ball)
and a process of dealing with obstacles (ie players of the
other team).

This formula shows the factors that are needed in order to be
successful. The obstacles can be internal or external.
Continuing the above analogy, if the player has a fear of
success, or a sore big toe, these can also prevent him
scoring.

A part of the monitoring process therefore is to ascertain
what obstacles there are for your client, and find ways to
deal with these obstacles if possible. Often simply an
awareness that an obstacle is there can shrink it. They often
take on unrealistic proportions until analysed.

Obstacles can be REMOVED, gone OVER, UNDER, AROUND or THROUGH, SHRUNK, or UTILISED.

Here are some examples:

- A client wants promotion, but doesn't get on with his boss, therefore can't get a reference. You find a way AROUND this obstacle by getting a reference from the HR department instead.
- A client wants to lose weight but can't stop eating chocolate. You REMOVE the obstacle by getting their partner to do the shopping so that there is no chocolate available (yes we know this is simplistic!)
- A client wants to enrol on a degree course but is terrified of rejection. You get THROUGH this obstacle by "feeling the fear and doing it anyway"
- A client wants to change career from being a lawyer to running a cattery but knows that her mother will not approve. You SHRINK this obstacle by working with the client on her adult status in relation to her mother.
- A client wants to improve their income but has chosen not to go out to work so that he is at home when the children come home from school or are ill. You UTILISE this obstacle by realising that this gives him 6 and a half hours of peace each day to plan and run an Internet accounting business.

Set backs

Another primary role of the coach is to be a support in times of set backs. You can envisage yourself as being ready to catch your client when they fall.

It is inevitable that if your clients are going for things, then sometimes things will go wrong. You need to

- Be positive
- Encourage
- Find ways to reframe
- Look for alternatives
- Listen to their disappointment/despair/anger without joining in

Stickability

By now you can probably write this section yourself!

Yes, you've got it: if you get all the bits right, stickability follows naturally.

However, this is one of the hardest processes in coaching, as although we might understand motivation and how, why and where it can break down, actually ensuring that motivation is maintained at a high level requires YOUR commitment and modelling of your motivation on their behalf and your ability to communicate this effectively.

Unlike in therapy, we cover this more closely in coaching by the use of contracts and also by being specific with the client as to their motivations and lack of same.

Giving answers/direction

This is an area of potential difficulty for all. Any students who come from a counselling background are likely to baulk at the idea of ever giving answers and direction, and it will depend on your hypnotherapy training, as well as your own natural inclinations as to how easy or difficult you will find it to get the right balance on this.

So let's set some parameters.

This process is for

- Tasking
- Helping a client to set goals
- Helping a client to monitor progress
- Challenging
- Creating accountability

It is NOT for

- Taking responsibility (as coach)
- Telling client what they "should" do
- Limiting options
- Imposing your values or opinions

Exercise

Do you think you will find it difficult to get the balance right? What problems do you perceive that you might encounter?

176

Creativity

The unconscious mind

As a Hypnotic Coach you have two of the most powerful things in the universe at your disposal in working with your client. Wow! That sounds good: and it is good: really good news for both of you!

And what are these two things?

Your unconscious and theirs!

We all use only a fraction of the potential of our mind; if we used just a little more, and believed in that potential just a little more just think of the benefit!

Here are a few hints for maximising the potential of the unconscious mind:

- The unconscious always has a positive aim for any behaviour, however negative it may seem.
- The unconscious does not understand negatives. Tell yourself not to think of a pink elephant: what do you think of?
- Whenever the unconscious mind concentrates on an idea, that idea becomes spontaneously realised. The unconscious mind cannot differentiate between something that is real and something that is imagined.
- The harder the mind tries to do something, the harder it will be: never ask a client to try to do something! The same applies to the word "hope".
- A strong emotion will always dominate a weaker one, so if you can attach a strong emotion to a goal, for instance, success becomes easier.
- The unconscious mind likes symbols, patterns and stories.

- The acceptance of one suggestion aids the acceptance of another. Sales people often use this technique; by getting you to say yes to unimportant questions, you are more likely to say yes to the big ones!
- The unconscious mind likes easier jobs first: almost as though it needs to be in training to work up to bigger tasks.
- The unconscious takes things personally: the rational mind is needed to, well, rationalise.
- The unconscious mind works on the principle of the least effort and will choose the path of least resistance.
- Repetition is needed to form a habit. Once installed the unconscious needs to be involved in its resolution.
- The unconscious works in the moment of now: if something is perceived as being true now, but reality shows a discrepancy, the unconscious will work to make reality fit the perception: hence visualising your future works!
- Just as the unconscious doesn't understand "try", so it doesn't interpret "going to be" as the conscious mind might imagine. If you decide that you are going to be a writer/artist/police officer/whatever, that is in the future, and your unconscious will keep it in the future until you choose to bring it into the present.

How to get ideas

Often your client will get stuck when asked how they might do something, or what they might do.

Here are some ways to help:

Brainstorm*

In a set amount of time come up with as many weird and wonderful ideas as possible, not giving any thought at all to reality.

For example:

If you were to spend a minute thinking of uses for a scratched and irreparable CD, you could come up with ideas such as

- A bird scarer
- A Christmas decoration
- Something on which to burn incense cones (don't try this one: I did, and the CD melted!)
- A Frisbee
- An ice-scraper
- To signal for rescue
- Earrings
- Print labels with photos of your favourite people and use as coasters

This could be extended by spending more time looking from different angles. Eg: What if you were a scientist, were lost in the jungle, were a child?

*some people feel that the word "brainstorm" is politically incorrect. If it bothers you feel free to use the word "mindshower" instead

Here's an example:

Coach: What subjects could you write about?

Client: Ummm. Cars. Motorbikes.

Coach: And what sort of sources would print these articles?

Client: Car magazines, men's magazines perhaps.

Coach: Spend one minute and tell me anything that you can think of, connected to cars and bikes you could write about, being as daft as you like:

Client: Lawnmowers, engines, caravans, cars that pull caravans, interiors, colours, why are colours so boring, mechanics, the AA, motorways, bike gear, motorway service stations, road signs, driving tests, failing tests, people who fail tests, racing cars, getting to race a car, how racing cars get to where they go, who organises it, who picks drivers, lorry driving, sleeping in a lorry park, statistics on accidents, day in the life of a paramedic, day in the life of an AA man. Gosh!

Coach: Let's go through these and see where they might be published:

Client: Home and Garden, Mechanics' trade magazine, Caravanning magazines, Newspapers, women's magazines, AA Members' magazine, Insurance companies' magazines, Service station guides, Consumer guides, Motor racing press, colour supplements, airline magazines.

Coach: so to start with you had two subjects and two sources and now you have 25 subjects and 14 sources.

Exercise

Practise brainstorming! Some people find it easy, others difficult to forget about the "realisticness" of what they are coming up with!

Forced Connections

Let's go straight into an example:

A client wants to find ways to make his wife happier as she has said she is fed up with him. He has decided to get home earlier, do more to help at home and take her out more. Now he is stuck.

Coach: look around the room you are in now and tell me three things you see:

Client: a notebook, a computer screen, a mug

Coach: Now how could the thought of a notebook connect with making your wife happy?

Client: I could write her poetry as I used to do

Coach: and how could a computer screen connect?

Client: we could watch a film together at home but make it as though it was at a cinema: popcorn, dark etc

Coach: and how could the mug connect?

Client: I could bring her a coffee in the morning.

This technique can be taken another step, by asking the client to be really outrageous in their thinking. In this case ask what he could do that would be so outrageous she would leave, or for a career based situation ask what might get them fired. Their ideas are then, of course, toned down!

Our client may suggest running down the street naked saying I love you, which can then be adapted into sending flowers with a soppy message attached, or spending all their savings on a holiday, which can be adapted to treating her to a luxury break.

At work, a client may think an outrageous way to get a pay rise would be to threaten the boss with violence, which can be adapted to writing a letter giving his reasons for deserving a rise.

The technique can also be used by finding a word to connect to by opening a dictionary at random.

15 ways to be more creative

1. Ask "what if" questions- the sillier the better, eg What if I paid myself a tip for every time I am nice to a client?
2. Use metaphors and analogies, eg my job is like a flooded river, it spills over into everything and that makes people angry.
3. Daydream, eg fantasise about being the boss and how everyone thinks you are wonderful
4. Pay attention to small ideas: from little acorns, great big oak trees grow
5. Use the Reverse Method, eg ask yourself, "how can I make less money?"
6. Play "just suppose", eg just suppose I got up half an hour earlier…
7. Use drawing, eg draw your position in the world and then explain your drawing to your coach, or draw a tree and explain why it is like you
8. Use the non-dominant hand occasionally
9. Ask your unconscious to solve a problem or answer a question for you overnight
10. Write poems about your life and goals
11. Use handwriting sometimes (with a nice pen and use colours) rather than the computer
12. Do sums, eg balance your cheque book without using a calculator or add up the value of your shopping as you go around the supermarket!
13. When you are part way through a novel or video, stop and think up your own ending
14. Do jigsaws and crosswords
15. Dance!

Specific issues

Careers

Many of your clients will be concentrating their efforts in the coaching relationship on improving their success and enjoyment within their career. This will take many forms, from someone in a menial job looking for something more fulfilling, to those who already, by conventional standards, would be seen as successes, but who want more.

All the techniques covered in this course can be used to help in career coaching, but let's look at some specific issues that relate to this area.

Firstly, people have very different expectations for themselves, but there will always be a limit to that expectation. This can be described as a wall, beyond which they are unlikely to go.

For one person, they may feel that the most they can achieve is a 3 bedroom semi, a Ford Focus, and a holiday in Spain every year. For someone else, they may feel they can become a millionaire, but would not imagine being a multi-millionaire.

It is vital, at the same time, to honour your client's beliefs, but encourage them to be stretched. It is also, as usual, important that you do not impose your values onto them. There are ways to assist your client to examine their self-imposed limits. Being qualified in hypnosis gives you an edge here in that you can utilise these skills to help your clients deal with their self-imposed limits.

In stating that your values should not be imposed on your client, it is also worth noting that your own limits will also affect your work. If you have a belief that, say, the love of money is the root of all evil, then this believe WILL affect your work with your clients until and unless you work it through.

Secondly, different things make different people happy, and this needs to be kept at the front of your awareness when working in career coaching. Any coaching in fact. The aim of the coach is to assist the client to reach the point where they are happy with the work they do, find it fulfilling, enjoy the processes they are involved in and feel appropriately rewarded.

Many people feel undervalued, their skills are wasted, they have missed opportunities, it is too late, or they are incompetent. They may also believe that work should not be enjoyed. That to enjoy what you are paid for is self-indulgent. Or they may feel they do not deserve more.

All of these things can be worked on: you are the catalyst to make the change!

Weight control

You will find that, when listing goals, a large number of your clients (particularly women) will include weight control as one of their aims. The priority that they give to it will vary, as will the amount by which they wish to reduce and the reasons why they wish to reduce.

Please note: the word "lose" should be avoided. Unconsciously this word is perceived as something to avoid. Throughout childhood the word is heard as a bad thing! (Don't lose your dinner money!). Loss is also, of course, linked to bereavement and failure so it is no wonder that the unconscious avoids losing! Use the words control and reduce instead.

Many people have self-limiting beliefs around weight. For example:

- All my family are big
- Whatever I do I can't lose weight (NB THEY WILL use the "L" word)
- I'm addicted to chocolate
- I have a slow metabolism

The crucial thing here is to get the client to a place of awareness that they can choose and take control. As a coach you can help them to analyse what they eat, but be careful not to get into the realms of advising them on their diet too specifically unless you are qualified to do so.

It is also important to be aware that food problems can be much more than just bad eating habits and can be tied into issues that need to be worked on in therapy. Such problems range from comfort eating through to anorexia and bulimia. As always, work within your bounds of competence and qualification. Some hypnotherapy qualifications will cover these in depth issues, others will not. If you are not qualified you may wish to seek out specialist training.

Remember however, that clients who come for coaching may not be willing to go down a therapeutic route however much YOU feel that they need to.

Case example

Paula was undergoing coaching at work, and at the initial session she stated the goal (among others) of losing three stone in weight. The coach worked with her using all the ideas in the goal setting section of this book, so Paula was very clear as to why she wanted to achieve the goal, and how she would do so.

But her weight did not reduce, and it turned out that her eating patterns were far worse that originally stated. She would regularly binge at midnight until 2am. The coach explained that this behaviour would need to be resolved before the process of eating correctly during the day, but Paula refused to "go there".

The coach was concerned that this might mean that in order to meet the goal, Paula might adopt extreme behaviours during the day. She expressed the concern, and for a while the relationship was shaky because of this. To date Paula has remained at the weight she started at.

Physical activity

Your clients are likely to include goals about fitness and activity in their plans. Once again they may have self limiting beliefs about this area, such as:

- I was never any good at sport
- I am too busy to exercise
- I hate exercise

Fiona Biddle has written a book (with her husband, Dr Stuart Biddle, an Exercise Psychologist) specifically for use by clients of hypnotherapists for weight control. The book gives lots of information to the "reluctant exerciser". It would be suitable for any of your clients who have activity or weight goals.

Alcohol

Clients will commonly say that they wish to drink less (and never more!). Be wary for any signs of dependence, and if these are found discuss referral to a suitably qualified therapist (presuming you do not have this specialist qualification) or medical practitioner.

Smoking

Another common goal is to stop smoking. As a qualified hypnotherapist you can offer to help, but be aware that a client may not want this, and if they want to use another method you need to be able to support them in this.

Sport performance

You are not a sports coach! (Well you might be: but not by virtue of reading this book). But you can still use your skills to help your client believe in their potential, to overcome fear of failure, and to stay motivated.

Case example

Bobby was a 110m hurdler, and chose his hypnotic coach because he particularly liked the idea of the mix. Of course, he had an athletics coach, but he felt he needed more. The remit was to help him to set goals for the next two seasons, to teach him techniques for concentration and to avoid fear in competitions and to address his work/life/sport balance.

The goal setting involved times to achieve, as well as training targets of duration, intensity and scope. The coach used hypnosis to work with confidence, focus, and particularly belief. Anchors were installed, utilising all modalities.

Finally, the coach helped Bobby determine choices around time spent on his different activities and helped him find ways to ensure that whichever mode he was in, he was truly IN that mode. Eg, if training, then he was training, and if he was with his girlfriend, then he was WITH HER.

Marketing your business

In order to make a business, you need the following factors:

1. A provider
2. A service or product
3. A purchaser

By virtue of reading this book (and we hope, taking the related qualification), you are working on number 1, turning yourself into a hypnotic coach, and 2, learning about the service you will be offering.

Both of these can be improved and developed indefinitely. Then there is number 3, and more specifically how to let the purchaser know that a) they need / want your service and b) you are there to provide it.

The element of competition also comes into this. How do you ensure that your potential purchaser believes that you are the best provider to purchase the service from?

All things for you to consider and plan for yourself.

The Income Formula

Income = value x difficulty x rarity x image x number of users

To illustrate this formula let's look at some examples:

H=High, M=Medium, L=Low

	Value	Difficulty	Rarity	Image	N Users	Income
David Beckham	H	H	H	H	H	H++++
Paul Scholes	H	H	H	L	H	H++
Plumber	H	M	M	M	L	M
Nurse	M	M	M	L	L	L
Cleaner	L	L	L	L	L	L

To explain: the perceived value of what Beckham does for his "users" is high, as is that of the plumber (you really need that washing machine!). Beckham might not find what he does difficult but most would, and few are so good at it. There are things which are rare but not difficult (eg being a sagger maker's bottom knocker), or difficult but not rare (eg counselling).

Image comes into the equation too. In the above table, the main difference between the income of Beckham and Scholes is down to image. The image of the role itself is also a factor. Finally the number of users impacts greatly on income. Take the example of the nurse. A nurse can only look after so many people at one time, and this limits the income dramatically.

As a final example let's look at Fire Fighters, who, at the time of writing this segment are threatening to strike for a 40% pay award. Why? (Other than that they want it!). Firstly, the role is much more difficult than it was when the pay structure was set up, and secondly (being controversial here!), the image of fire fighters and the perceived value of what they do has been boosted dramatically by September 11.

So, how does this affect you as a coach? Simply to maximise each element of the formula. Of course, whether you choose to find ways to maximise the "N users" element is a choice. You may prefer to work one to one and not too many hours, and so concentrate your efforts on the other elements.

And remember, these are all perceptions, and it is the perceptions of your "users" that need to be maximised.

Exercise

When you see people in different roles, see how they could maximise their income using this formula.

How could you maximise yours?

Advertising

This is an area where many involved in human change make errors. It is a mistake to believe that one only needs to become a hypnotic coach and business will just roll in. In order to ensure that people know you exist you must advertise.

However, one must be cautious; claims of high success made by the sellers of advertising must be looked at with suspicion. As a rule of thumb, if the advertiser contacts you in the first instance, chances are you will not want to be using their service. One only need look at Yellow Pages, who will contact you once when you set up your business, but if you choose not to advertise, they leave it with you to make the first move.

The difficulty with hypnotic coaching is that there is not a directory subsection for it, so Coaches need to make their best possible match. We would recommend that you avoid the Therapist Section of the Yellow Pages, as we have conducted some informal research and have discovered that there is very little traffic for this section. We would suggest that you utilise either the hypnotherapy, counselling or psychotherapy section for your Yellow Pages Ad. We say this because in many ways, coaching is a re-branding of Psychotherapy and Counselling. So as these are the nearest disciplines to Coaching, it is logical to advertise there so that those who would look to seek out this for of intervention can find you. Please note, unless you have a specialist qualification in Counselling or Psychotherapy do not advertise yourself as a Psychotherapist or Counsellor. By all means call yourself a Certified Hypnotic Coach IF you have the certificate to prove it.

There are also other locations to advertise in which can also be very effective. One must bear in mind that successful

194

people are your main clients. This in many ways differs from traditional therapy. Therapy can be seen as being a sign of failure, whilst successful people are more than happy to acknowledge that they have a personal coach. We would recommend advertising in "What's On" type magazines. This is because the people who tend to buy these publications are middle class and well educated with disposable income. These qualities are often those of a typical coaching client. Advertising in this medium need not be expensive; here is a sample of a successful ad:

Hypnotic Coaching:
Conducted by Certified Hypnotic Coach
Call for free literature or appointment
Shaun Brookhouse, MA, CPC
0161 881 1677
www.hypno-nlp.com

As you can see, this linage ad will cost very little, yet convey the necessary information which prospective clients will need. One should not give loads of information in an advertisement. People who are interested in Coaching know what it can do, so they will not require an education in the ad. For those who do not they can use your literature to assist in their decision making process.

Also, mention coaching in any hypnotherapy ads. We have found that many clients coming for "ordinary" hypnotherapy choose us because of the inclusion of coaching, with its forward thinking perception.

As you will be charging more for coaching services than perhaps you are charging for therapy, (eg one of the authors charges £50/£75 per session for therapy and £250 per month for coaching) the use of directed mailings or leaflet insertions in specific publications may prove useful.

Here is a formula to follow:

Mail shot formula

3% is a terrific response

2% is very good

1% is acceptable

For example, if your fees are £176.25 per month.

Out of 10 clients

2 book for 2 months=£705.00 less VAT
5 book for 4 months=£3525.00 less VAT
3 book for 6 months=£3172.50 less VAT

Total income £7402.50
Each client is worth £740.25

Sending out 1000 pieces of mail costs:
Printing   £300
Postage   £370
Labels   £40
TOTAL COST £710

If you get a
3% response= 30 clients @£740.25 = £21497.50
2% response= 20 clients @£740.25 = £14095
1% response = 10 clients @£740.25= £6692.50

Mail shots only work if what you are selling is a product with a reasonably high value. Many in therapy have tried mail shots which failed because at say each client being worth £100, you would need to send many thousands of pieces to generate a reasonable return. We did not include in the costing your time in envelope stuffing, but figure for a 1000 piece mail shot, you will be spending the better part of a day and a half stuffing, you need to factor in your hourly rate to give a true picture of the costs.

How to Write an Advertisement:

1. Print advertising is the form most often used and used incorrectly

2. Ads should make you want to buy.

3. Ads should be easy to understand

4. Ads should be eye-catching and easy to read. Ads should provide enough information so that people know what to do to buy. Always give a response mechanism

5. DO NOT USE CAPITALS THROUGHOUT: THEY ARE JUST NOT AS READABLE!

The Internet

This is probably the best source of new coaching clients you will have. It is imperative for Hypnotic Coaches to have their own web presence. This should not be left to chance, unless you have a flair for design, get a professional to develop your site.

There are ways to keep the costs of this down. Keep away from really flashy sites which take ages to down load. If the site does not appear in total within 3-5 seconds, people will move on to another site. Also, ensure there is enough information to let people know that you know what you are talking about. We would also recommend that you have a separate presence for your coaching practice from your therapy practice; by all means link the two up but have them as separate entities.

Public Relations

What is the need for PR? Well if people do not know you exist, then they will not come to you. PR comprises everything you do, including advertising, your presentation material, etc. By presentation materials we mean brochures, business cards and stationary. Finally one markets oneself through everything one does. That is to say, the way you carry yourself both in sessions and out in public is very important but so too is the way you answer the phone, how prompt you are in sending materials. People who request information from our practice get it within 24 hours. Clients like this attention to detail which may seem unimportant, but here in the UK we are not used to customer service and for us to succeed, customer service must be our credo.

Lecturing

The idea of going out to the public and talking about Hypnotic Coaching is the best and least expensive way to build up a practice. When Shaun came to the UK in 1991, he spent 3 days a week giving talks to anyone who would listen. He would book local libraries, go to companies and finally approach service clubs. Service clubs are organisations like the Lions, the Rotary, the WI, etc. These organisations are always looking for interesting speakers to talk to their groups. As a Hypnotic Coach, you are certainly an interesting speaker. As a rule this is the way we run public talks, which by the way, if you are running them for free at the local library, the library will give you the room for free and publicise it as a public service.

1. **Demonstrate on a member of the audience if appropriate.** Many of the techniques used in coaching can be adapted for demonstrational purposes.

2. **Discuss what coaching isn't and what hypnosis isn't.** You would be surprised at the lack of public understanding of coaching and hypnosis. It is important to emphasise that it is not psychotherapy or counselling, but a process which helps get the best out of people in a similar way that athletic coaches get the best out of their athletes.

3. **Detail the benefits of Hypnotic Coaching.** After telling them what it isn't tell them what it is, how to use it, who uses it. Discuss in great detail the benefits of coaching. Personal copy is very good at this point so if you can disclose how coaching has helped you personally, this is the time to discuss it.

5. **Answering questions.** This is the lion's share of your talk. Get the audience to ask you specific questions. If they do not, ask yourself one or two questions to get the ball rolling.

This is the outline for a 60 minute talk; steps 1-3 should take 40 mins while step 4 should take 20 mins.

Writing

Another excellent, and free way to get the word out about your practice is to write articles for magazines and newspapers about coaching in all its forms.

1. **Publications to write for**. This depends on the angle of your article, we have written articles on coaching for women's magazines, style mags, executive coaching for management and sales mags. Go to your local library or to the internet to do a search for the various titles that are currently in print. Be aware, that for certain publications like women's magazines, they are article starved. What we mean by this is that the editors are constantly looking for articles to fill their publication.

2. **Get practice details mentioned in the article**. This is your payment. Most editors do not pay for articles so as part of the deal you ensure that at the end you have something like this: Shaun Brookhouse MA, CPC is a Certified Hypnotic Coach in the Greater Manchester area, he can be reached at 0161 882 0400 or enquiries@hypno-manchester.com.

3.   **Subjects to write on.** The possibilities here are endless, and again dependent on the publication you are writing for at the time. We suggest that you write the article, then when completed, you decide which publication will be most interested in the subject matter you wrote on. It is much easier than trying to write for a publication specifically.

Referrals

One of the main ways to be successful with Hypnotic Coaching is to ensure that those whom you coach become referral generators for you and your practice. Here are the five steps in being able to do this:

1. **Success**: For a client to be a good referral generator, one must first have been successful in their time with you. In rare occasions I have had people refer to me even though they themselves have not been successful, but this is definitely the exception as opposed to the rule.

2. **Rapport**: We say that rapport is the key to all therapeutic interventions, it is the same for generating referrals. Without rapport there is no desire for the client to refer.

3. **Make client comfortable with coaching:** As with many techniques of personal development, there is the possibility that the client will not be happy with discussing the fact that they have had coaching. For clients like this it is imperative to discuss all of the benefits that have been experienced whilst the client was with you as well as mentioning places where coaching has had good press. Finally, it is no

201

bad thing to mention celebrities who have benefited from coaching. This makes an unconscious association with the client and the celebrity which will make them far more likely to want to discuss coaching with others.

4. **Socially skilled client**: There is no point in having the first three without this one. Whilst a client may have been successful with you, the rapport is good, and the individual is totally comfortable with coaching, if the client has no friends or colleagues they will not be a good referral generator. However, for those who fall into this category, perhaps with the skills they learned with you, they will interact more comfortably with others. Should this happen this client is an excellent source for new clients.

5. **Ask for the referrals**: Sounds basic, but we often do not do this most important step. We know of a client who referred to another coach simply because he thought his coach was too busy to see anyone else. One can do this step professionally like "When people see how well you are getting on, I would appreciate your recommendation". One does not have to overkill this, mention it only once or twice or you will appear desperate.

Personality and Props

1. **Telephone**: Reliability is a must here, without the phone you are dead. Panasonic or BT are the most reliable we have found (but they don't work when dropped in the bath so keep a cheap alternative available for emergencies!)

   - **Answering the phone:** Salutation and identification is important here, most people miss the first 3 seconds of a call. Good Morning followed by your name or trading name may be adequate. Never simply say hello or quote a telephone number. However, do not have a long intro as people find this frustrating.

   - **Answering machine/call waiting/divert:** Answering machine as above. We recommend both call waiting and divert to avoid missing calls. However, if you are having call divert to a mobile make sure the mobile message is the same as the office message. People do not like to think they are calling a mobile even if you are paying for the call

2. **Office**

   - **How should it look:** As a rule if you work from home make your home look like an office and if at an office make the office look like home

   - **What does it say about you?** It must exude confidence and your professionalism

3. **Business plan**: Make monthly plans and stick to them. Use coaching techniques to help you!

4. **Business forecast/budget/targets/goals** Do every 3,6,9, and 12 months

5. **Time management**: Be a model of excellence. Many times clients are seeking your help for time management. Get a system that works for you and stick to it. No EXCEPTIONS!

Other promotional ideas

- Offer free workshops on aspects of Hypnotic Coaching.

- Offer promotions to members of health or sports clubs, eg motivation for fitness

- Offer sessions for schools, hand out brochures and the kids can market you to their parents. (Be careful about the use of hypnosis: you would need specific written permission from parents)

- Use yourself and your car as an advertising medium. Wendi Friesen put a sign in her car saying Hypnogolf when she went to watch a tournament: she got two new clients! You could even get a baseball hat saying "Hypnotic Coach".

- Talk loudly about what you do whenever there are people around, and have business cards ready.

- Get extra referrals by offering a free session for a friend

- Target special interest groups or specific types of company. Don Mottin runs stress management classes specifically for hairdressers or taxi drivers. The class is the same but they feel they are special. You could offer coaching for the construction industry, or for accountants in private practice.

- Produce CDs with a brief introduction to coaching and give them out as you would business cards.

- Write newsletters and post to current and ex clients.

- Use a photo in your publicity. If you only speak with a client on the phone it can be very important for visual people to know what you look like. (You may also need to know what they look like, but if they are not visual they may not understand why!)

- Send a thank you note to a client for a referral, but only when you've checked that is ok with your new client!

- Call radio stations. Almost any topic can be adapted to the subject of coaching.

The coach's personal development

To be a successful coach you need to:

- Look after yourself
- Care for your clients
- Want to support your clients
- Believe that you can make a difference
- Recognise that, as you help a client, that will have a knock on effect to improve the lives of those around them, and so on
- Be willing to develop
- Be willing to accept your faults and work on them
- Be willing to take risks
- Be a life long learner
- Believe that you ARE a Hypnotic Coach (NOW!)
- Give 100% when you are coaching (there is a huge difference between 99 and 100%), and let go when you are not!
- Develop tools and skills constantly
- Practise, and use the tools on yourself
- Have confidence in your ability to give to others
- Consider developing areas of specialism
- Have coaching yourself, or get a mentor
- Ensure that you have people to offload onto or to ask for advice
- Learn from your clients

Ideas

The majority of the population in the Western world just "exist" from Monday to Friday in order to live at weekends. The same applies to holidays.

How would it be to try to live a "five nines" happy life? That's 99.999%!

Goals can be seen in five categories: the Five Fs:

- Family
- Fitness
- Friends
- Finance
- Faith (in yourself)

If you believe you can, or if you believe you can't: you are right!

Motivation can be eeeeeeeasy: do it with eeeeeeeease:

Education	Excellence
Entertainment	Experience
Enthusiasm	Example
Encouragement	Energy

FEAR = **F**alse **E**xpectation of **A**nticipated **R**eality

Or

FEAR = **F***** **E**verything **A**nd **R**un

Or

FEAR = **F**alse **E**vidence **A**ppearing **R**eal

Or

FEAR = **F**orever **E**xpecting **A**wful **R**esults

Or

FEAR = **F**ace it **E**valuate it **A**nalyse it **R**eject it

Q: What is the most stressful job in the world?
A: Whatever your client does for a living!

<u>S</u>elf help
<u>U</u>nderstanding
<u>C</u>larity
<u>C</u>ourage
<u>E</u>steem
<u>S</u>elf-confidence
<u>S</u>elf-image

<u>F</u>rustration
<u>A</u>nger
<u>I</u>rritability
<u>L</u>ack of goals
<u>U</u>ncertainty
<u>R</u>esentment
<u>E</u>mptiness

"If you have to eat a frog, don't look at it too long" – Mark Twain

"If we do not change direction, we are liable to end up where we are headed"

"Stop analysing, hoping, wishing....and most of all.... Stop complaining!" -Wendi Friesen

"The best way to predict the future is to invent it." - unknown

"If it's to be, it's up to me" - unknown

"Take calculated risks. That is quite different from being rash." - George S. Patton

"Happiness happens when your conscious is not dominated by addictions and demands and you just experience life as a parade of preferences" - Ken Keyes Jnr.

"A happy person is not a person in a certain set of circumstances but rather a person with a certain set of attitudes" -Hugh Downs

"Everything that is worthwhile in life is scary. Choosing a school, choosing a career, getting married, having kids--all those things are scary. If it is not fearful, it is not worthwhile." -Paul Tornier

"When I hear somebody sigh, 'Life is hard,' I am always tempted to ask, 'Compared to what?'" -Sydney J. Harris

"he U.S. Constitution doesn't guarantee happiness, only the pursuit of it. You have to catch up with it yourself." - Benjamin Franklin

"Do you know a good recipe for longevity? ... Always be sure to get up in the morning. And you can ensure that by drinking a lot of water before you go to bed" - Jeffrey Zeig

"A goal is not the same as a desire, and this is an important distinction to make. You can have a desire you don't intend to act on. But you can't have a goal you don't intend to act on." - Tom Morris

"A winner is someone who recognizes his God-given talents, works his tail off to develop them into skills, and uses these skills to accomplish his goals." – Larry Bird

"Keep away from people who try to belittle your ambitions. Small people always do that, but the really great make you feel that you, too, can become great." – Mark Twain

"If I try to be like him, who will be like me?" - Yiddish proverb

"Courage is not the towering oak that sees storms come and go; it is the fragile blossom that opens in the snow." - Alice Mackenzie Swaim

"Obstacles are those frightful things you see when you take your eyes off the goal." - Henry Ford, Founder of Ford Motor Company

"We will receive not what we idly wish for but what we justly earn. Our rewards will always be in exact proportion to our service." - Earl Nightingale

"I don't know the key to success, but the key to failure is trying to please everybody." - Bill Cosby

"Not a shred of evidence exists in favor of the idea that life is serious." - Brendan Gill

"Heroes are not there to be copied. They are there to inspire us to be different and better." - unknown

"Your dreams are like a rolling sense of destination. They are the other side of the horizon, a never-ending story. To reach them you must see limits as perceptions, not as realities. Dreams, then, are milestones on a journey without a final destination. Don't stop dreaming." - Frank Dick

"If I won't be myself, who will?" - Alfred Hitchcock

"In order to be a realist you must believe in miracles." - David Ben Gurion

"Perfection is the dream: the fight to get there is the reality."
- Ferrari mechanic's motto

"Why have dreams if you are not prepared to keep
appointments with them?"   - Frank Dick

"If we all worked on the assumption that what is accepted as
true is really true, there would be little hope for advance." -
Orville Wright

"Freedom is what you do with what's been done to you" -
Jean-Paul Sartre

"You can't stop the waves, but you can learn to surf." -
Unknown

"To control attention means to control experience, and
therefore the quality of life." - Mihaly Csikszentmihalyi

"The only man who can't change his mind is one who hasn't
got one." - Edward Noyes Westcot

"Restlessness and discontent are the first necessities of
progress" - Edison

"No man really becomes a fool until he stops asking
questions." – Charles Steinmetz

"Better keep yourself clean and bright; you are the window through which you must see the world." - George Bernard Shaw

"You must be prepared to get out of the comfort and security of the nest if you are to learn how to fly" - Frank Dick

"To look at something as though we had never seen it before requires great courage." - Henri Matisse

"If you can't be a good example, then you'll just have to be a horrible warning." - Catherine Aird

"Holding anger is like grasping a hot coal with the intent of throwing it at someone else; you are the one who gets burned."
- The Buddha

"Normal is someone whom you don't know very well" - Anon

"When your desires are strong enough you will appear to possess superhuman powers to achieve." - Napoleon Hill

"Big goals get big results. No goals get no results or somebody else's results." - Mark Victor Hansen

"Keep the faculty of effort alive in you by a little gratuitous exercise every day." - William James

"Optimism is essential to achievement and it is also the foundation of courage and of true progress." - Nicholas Murray Butler

"A goal is not the same as a desire, and this is an important distinction to make. You can have a desire you don't intend to act on. But you can't have a goal you don't intend to act on." - Tom Morris

"if you want security go to jail!" - Anthony Robbins

"Other people's opinion of you does not have to become your reality." - Les Brown

"Successful people ask better questions, and as a result, they get better answers." - Anthony Robbins

"Dream big, not small. Small dreams aren't worth getting out of bed for." - Frank Dick

"How committed are you? There is a remarkable difference between 99% and 100%!" - Vic Conant

" The only things in life you ever really regret, are the chances you didn't take....to hell with the consequences!" - Unknown

"If you don't push yourself to the limit, how do you know where the limit is?"
- Unknown

"People often say that motivation doesn't last. Well, neither does bathing - that's why we recommend it daily." - Zig Ziglar

"The day the child realizes that all adults are imperfect he becomes an adolescent; the day he forgives them, he becomes an adult; the day he forgives himself, he becomes wise." - Aiden Nowlan

"There may be more to learn from climbing the same mountain a hundred times than by climbing a hundred different mountains." - Richard Nelson

"Forgiveness means giving up all hope of a better past." - Landrum Bolling

"You miss 100 percent of all the shots you never take. " -Wayne Gretzky

"Good people are good because they've come to wisdom through failure. We get very little wisdom from success, you know." - William Saroyan

"Desire is the key to motivation, but it's the determination and commitment to an unrelenting pursuit of your goal, a commitment to excellence, that will enable you to attain the success you seek." - Unknown

"When you get to the end of your rope, tie a knot and hang on." - Franklin D. Roosevelt

"There are only two lasting bequests we can give our children... one is roots, the other wings."
- Stephen Covey

"There is no scarcity of opportunity to make a living at what you love to do, there is only scarcity of resolve to make it happen."
- Wayne Dyer

"Why cry if you can laugh? Why wait if you can act? Get out there - make a difference!" - Unknown

"Your own mind is a sacred enclosure into which nothing harmful can enter except by your permission."
- Ralph Waldo Emerson

"You may have a fresh start any moment you choose, for this thing that we call "failure" is not the falling down, but the staying down."
- Mary Pickford

"We can all dream and be creative. In an instant a two year old can turn a cardboard box into a spaceship a submarine, a time machine. We have all been two year olds at least once. We are all creative, we are all dreamers." - Frank Dick

"The art of being wise is the art of knowing what to overlook."
- William James

"We must walk consciously only part way toward our goal and then leap in the dark to our success."
- Henry David Thoreau

"Reduce your plan to writing... The moment you complete this, you will have definitely given concrete form to the intangible desire."
- Napoleon Hill

"Aim for success not perfection... Remember that fear always lurks behind perfectionism. Confronting your fears and allowing yourself the right to be human can, paradoxically, make you a far happier and more productive person."
- Dr. David Burns

"Envy can be a positive motivator. Let it inspire you to work harder for what you want." - Robert Bringle

"Some people] have a wonderful capacity to appreciate again and again, freshly and naively, the basic goods of life, with awe, pleasure, wonder, and even ecstasy." - A.H. Maslow

"Quality is remembered long after the price is forgotten". - Gucci family motto

"Your life is more like a decathlon than a single event. Sometimes you have to work to be better at one event in order to be able to improve in another. Every event helps your total score." - Frank Dick

Resources

Our own websites: www.ukacdemy.org

If you are looking for a coach in your area go to
www.elifecoach.org

Sedona method resources, available from www.lifetools.com

If you are not already a member, we recommend that you
join the National Council for Hypnotherapy: 0845 076 3724 or
visit www.hypnotherapists.org.uk

For hypnosis information outside the UK contact the National
Guild of Hypnotists www.ngh.net

If you are interested in hypnosis podcasts you can visit
www.hypnosiscast.co.uk

Coaching website: www.coachville.com

For buying used books on line: www.2ndhand.org.uk

Appendix A

Code of Ethics and Practice for Coaching from the UK Academy

All coaches should undertake to adhere to the following code:

1. Client Welfare
The welfare of the client is the primary concern of the coach. It should only take second place if not to put it first would seriously jeopardise other members of the public or the coach's welfare.

2. Confidentiality
Confidentiality is to be maintained in all but the most exceptional circumstances. These can only include: legal action (criminal or civil court cases where a court order is made demanding disclosure - includes coroner's courts) and where there is good cause to believe that not to disclose would cause danger of serious harm to others. Most standards of confidentiality applied in professional contexts are based on the Common Law concept of confidentiality where the duty to keep confidence is measured against the concept of "greater good". A stronger form as advocated, may be provided by the use of a written contract containing a confidentiality clause. The sharing of anonymous case histories with supervisors and peer-support groups is not a breach of professional confidentiality. The sharing of open case histories with supervisors is also not a breach. Feedback to referring employers etc. can only take the form of general comments as to progress (and then with permission); specific details should be kept confidential.

3. Service

Coaches will only offer services in areas in which they have demonstrated their competence, in other words, in which they have a meaningful qualification. They have a responsibility to provide the client with the best possible service available and in the event of the extent of their skills being exceeded, onwards referral to a therapist or medical practitioner who may offer such a service.

4. Development of 'Skill-base'

Coaches are required to maintain or improve their level of skills and professional competence by:
a. undertaking formal continuing training, by attending workshops, courses and seminars, AND
b. sharing of experiences and exploring such with supervisors/peer-support groups

They should also maintain an awareness of research and developments in the field of Coaching, Hypnosis and other linked fields.

5. Exploitation

All exploitation is abuse!

Coaches shall not behave in any manner that shall give rise to the exploitation of a client. They shall not enter into any other relationship, outside the professional relationship, while within a contractual arrangement with a client. They shall make their charges known to the client before coaching is commenced. They shall not accept any inappropriate gifts, gratuities or favours from a client. Should at any time a relationship, other than as described above, develop between a client and coach, then the client shall be referred on to another competent coach, at the earliest time commensurate with the welfare of the client and in any case, no further fees shall be taken.

6. Advertising

Advertising, no matter in what form or medium it is placed, shall represent a true picture of the coach, their skill base, qualifications, facilities and any benefits that may be expected from coaching and shall conform to current Advertising Law.

7. General Conduct

Coaches shall not behave in any manner, within or outside the context of coaching, that would undermine the public's confidence in the profession or bring the profession into disrepute. This includes a failure to act appropriately when they become aware of another coach's unethical activity, improper use of skills, criminal conviction, misbehaviour towards other professionals, discrimination on the basis of ethnic or sexual factors or anything that is the subject of any civil judgement regarding neglect of duty of care. They are obliged to advise clients of appropriate avenues of complaint.

In practise coaches should follow these principles:

1. Professional Indemnity Insurance.

This is a prerequisite for any coach to practise and must be maintained by the practitioner. It is recommended that it should be an agreed adequate minimum cover.
They should also respect all other professionals' status and the boundaries of their professional remit.

2. Respect

All coaches should respect other coaches, and other professionals

3. Provision of a Contract

All coaching is undertaken as a result of a contract between the client and the coach. This should be a written contract.

Such a contract should include statements of cost per session or whole course of therapy, confidentiality, the client's right of access to the complaints procedure of the coach's membership body and the fact that there can be no guarantee of specific results. The inclusion of a clause that defines the scope of confidentiality within coaching raises it from a Common Law duty to Contractual Limitation and duty to deliver. (Thus it becomes easier for all parties to understand their rights and duties within the relationship and lowers any risk of abuse or misunderstanding.)

5. Maintenance of Records/Notes and Recording Sessions.
It is recommended that case notes should be maintained to include personal details, history, program of coaching(as agreed between client and coach) and a copy of the contract, as well as session/progress notes. These should be maintained as hard copy and any use of computer records should be with the client's agreement and within the terms of the Data Protection Act. Audio and video recording (with time coded tracking) of sessions are a safeguard to all parties in respect of abuse and false allegations of such, as well as being an aid to recording the process of coaching. As such coaches can choose to make these a routine procedure but this must be disclosed to clients and carried out with their advised consent.

6. Display of Credentials
Only valid qualifications and certificates issued in respect of relevant courses or training events or certificates of registration/accreditation as issued by professional governing bodies may be displayed. The display of testimonials is considered unprofessional, although they can be shared, discretely, with prospective clients.

Special issues:

a. Misuse of the Title 'Doctor'

No coach shall use the title 'Doctor' in a manner that may mislead any member of the public to believe they are medically qualified, if they are not so qualified. Any use of the title must be clearly defined by a qualifying statement, i.e. the form of the doctorate.

b. Clients Under the Age of Majority/Consent or with Special Needs.

Coaches shall only deal with clients under the age of majority/consent or with special needs, after obtaining consent of an appropriate adult (parent or legal guardian). All sessions shall be conducted in the presence of an appropriate adult (parent, guardian or agreed adult third party) OR recorded on time indexed video format.

Appendix B

Training in hypnotherapy

Shaun and Fiona's school, the UK Academy of Therapeutic Arts and Sciences has a hypnotherapy practitioner course which runs at several centres throughout the UK.

The course is accredited by the National Council for Hypnotherapy and includes the nationally accredited Hypnotherapy Practitioner Diploma.

For further information, see www.hypno-nlp.org and www.hypnotherapists.org.uk

Index

Lightning Source UK Ltd.
Milton Keynes UK
21 May 2010

154475UK00002B/21/A